THE
PATCHWORK PILGRIMAGE

THE PATCHWORK PILGRIMAGE

How to Create Vibrant Church Decorations
and Vestments with Quilting Techniques

JILL LIDDELL

With Historical Essays by
ANDREW LIDDELL

VIKING STUDIO BOOKS

For our grandchildren—
Olivia and Samantha Holcroft,
Emma, Holly, and Laura Clifton-Brown,
Marcus and Caitlin Liddell—
with all our love

NOTE TO THE READER

All scriptural quotations in this book have been taken from the New International Version of the Bible unless otherwise indicated.

VIKING STUDIO BOOKS

Published by the Penguin Group
Penguin Books USA Inc., 375 Hudson Street,
New York, New York, 10014, U.S.A.

Penguin Books Ltd, 27 Wrights Lane,
London W8 5TZ, England

Penguin Books Australia Ltd, Ringwood,
Victoria, Australia

Penguin Books Canada Ltd, 2801 John Street,
Markham, Ontario, Canada L3R 1B4

Penguin Books (N.Z.) Ltd, 182-90 Wairau Road,
Auckland 10, New Zeland

Penguin Books Ltd, Registered Offices:
Harmondsworth, Middlesex, England

First published by Viking Studio Books, an imprint of Penguin Books USA Inc.

First printing, October, 1993
10 9 8 7 6 5 4 3 2 1

Library of Congress
Catalog Card Number: 93-85068

Book designed by Marilyn Rey
Printed and bound by Dai Nippon Printing Co., Ltd., Tokyo, Japan

ISBN: 0-525-93689-0 (cloth); ISBN: 0-525-48615-1 (paperback)

Contents

Preface

What began as a quest for information about the early church and its vestments soon became a pilgrimage, and I find that I have joined a movement that is not only worldwide and gathering momentum all the time, but is also opening up new quilting horizons and creating new opportunities for patchworkers everywhere.

It is a movement that is overturning tradition and challenging old concepts of design, but it actually began some three thousand years ago in the Sinai Desert when Moses, seeking materials for the Tabernacle, said to the Israelites, "All who are skilled among you are to make everything the Lord has commanded...[and] every skilled woman spun with her hands and brought what she had spun..." (Exodus 10:10 and 25).

In the following pages you will see how "skilled" women from all over the world are interpreting this command today by employing patchwork and quilting techniques to create visually exciting furnishings to beautify their churches.

Patchwork and appliqué have the advantage of covering large surfaces quickly and cheaply, and because of the desire by church authorities to commission colorful contemporary designs that are in tune with the more relaxed attitude to worship and the need to involve the congregation in the life of the church, the quiltmaker's craft has been elevated to a new form of liturgical art. You will also discover that patchwork, and the recycling of fabrics, are by no means newcomers to the church!

I was helped in my pilgrimage by many people: first and foremost my thanks go to Her Majesty, Queen Margrethe II of Denmark, and her sister, Princess Benedikte, for graciously allowing me to feature their beautiful work; to Lisbet Borggreen, who worked so hard to obtain the photographs of the royal vestments and also introduced me to all the other Danish artists; and to Birthe Ravn who so kindly translated information about the royal vestments into English. In England, I was set on my way by two ecclesiastical designers, Beryl Dean and Jane Lemon, who generously gave me the names of many English artists; by Geoffrey Jolly, M.B.E., who helped me with information about fabrics, as did the British Textile Technology Group in Manchester; by Pamela J. McDowall who lent me her workbooks; by Sheila Betterton; by Elizabeth Ingram, the editor of *Thread of Gold— The Embroideries and Textiles in York Minster*; by Anne Wynne-Wilson and Margaret H. Simpson of the Quaker Tapestry Scheme, who both provided considerable help and information; and by Jenni Dobson, who generously gave her time and her talents and made many useful suggestions, as always.

In the United States and Canada, I owe grateful thanks to the many members of the quilt guilds; to Barbara Coombs, Marty Bowne, editor of *American Quilter* magazine, Yuko Watanabe, Professor Nancy-Lou Patterson, Helen Bradfield of Create & Celebrate Canada, and Deborrah Sherman, editor of *Canada Quilts*, for putting me in touch with liturgical artists over there; and to the Reverend Dr. Robert G. Carroon of the Episcopal Diocese of Connecticut for providing valuable help and information about early vestments. In Australia, I would especially like to thank Barbara Holmes and her brother and sister-in-law, Dr. Edward Mickleburgh and his wife June, for nobly tracking down information and photographs during Barbara's visit to Canberra, and for their valuable help later. Thanks also go to Ruth Hingston for her help.

But my main vote of thanks must go to members of our church in London: to the Vicar, the Reverend Ian Kitteringham and his wife Jeanette for their support and encouragement throughout the project (Ian lent us half his library to do the necessary research); to Barbara Holmes and Gill Bryan for drawing patterns and diagrams; and to the other members of the Sewing Guild of St. Mary Magdalene: Pauline Charlton, Barbara Hill, Jean Hills, Kay Griffin, Jill Jeffery, Kitty King, Dora Littlechild, and Violet Plume.

Finally, nothing would have been achieved without the help of my wonderful husband Andrew, who not only advised (and consoled!) but also researched and wrote all the historical sections of the book, and of my editor, Cyril I. Nelson, who gave me his usual unstinting support and encouragement.

JILL LIDDELL

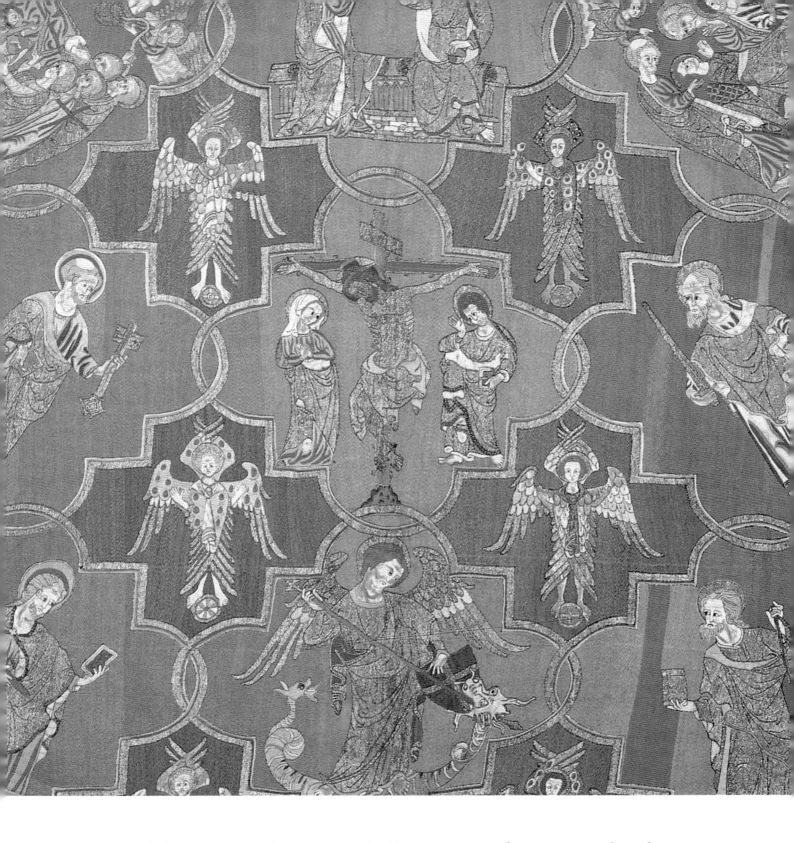

A Pilgrim's Guide to the Origins of the Church and Vestments

A pilgrimage is a journey of discovery undertaken for religious motives, and people from all nations and all religions have set out on pilgrimages since time began.

In this book, we take you on a journey of discovery to show you how women from all over the world are using patchwork techniques to glorify God either in the form of vestments, altar furnishings, or banners in churches of many different denominations, or simply as meditative pieces for personal use. The book is set out in geographical sections as a sort of atlas for pilgrims, so that you can draw inspiration from distant sources and see how the Holy Spirit works through our fingers across all frontiers.

Patchwork in the broadest sense has tremendous relevance to the decoration of churches today. In the past, in largely agricultural communities there were long periods of enforced idleness, rare public events, no football or baseball games, no movies, few theaters, no television. Crafts were a pastime and the churches ready patrons. Embroideries, mosaics, frescoes, plaster work, carvings—the most elaborate and time-consuming processes were used to decorate churches, and they glorify many old churches and cathedrals to this day. But in modern times leisure activities and entertainments have supplanted crafts; laborious processes have become a chore or an eccentricity, and many churches languish cold and unadorned, particularly in Europe with its historical oversupply. Here is patchwork's opportunity to fill a decorative void and fill a spiritual need.

FORTY FEET OF SPACE

Such a decorative void was the challenge that faced Nancy-Lou Patterson, a professor of fine art at Waterloo University, Ontario, Canada, and a noted liturgical artist. She was asked by St. Peter's Lutheran Church in Kitchener, Ontario, if she would design something to decorate a huge blank wall of gray limestone behind the main altar. "Awed, I gazed at the forty feet of space soaring up before me," she said at an address she gave at an ecumenical service held during *Quilt Canada 1987/Le Salon National de la Courtepoint 1987* in Montreal. "Then a thought came: why not design a wall hanging...based upon the principles of quilt construction, a subject with which I had become familiar through my research and collecting of Waterloo County Mennonite quilts."[1] The giant hanging (fig. 1), which is the size of three queen-size quilts attached end to end, was made for her by the Mennonite craftspeople who made quilts for the Sap Bucket, which is operated by Karla Kraus and Pam Sittler in Elmira, Ontario. This commission led Nancy-Lou to use quilting techniques in more of her work, and three of her fine pieces can be seen in the Canadian section of this book.

Another artist faced with a similar challenge was Beverley Shore Bennett from New Zealand whose preferred medium is stained glass, but who found that an enormous pieced dossal that she designed and made for St. Paul's Cathedral in Wellington "has brought more comment than any window I have ever designed." This dossal can be seen in figure 109.

Patchwork offers a wonderful way to decorate economically large areas that would require a huge expenditure of time or money if undertaken by any other decorative art or craft. But before looking further at work being done today, let us cast an eye backward to see how furnishings and vestments developed in the early church and how some of the more familiar Christian images came into existence.

THE FIRST CHRISTIAN BANNERS

In the year A.D. 312, General Constantine, governor of the northern provinces of the Roman Empire, marched against Italy with the support of the army to claim the imperial throne from his rival Maxentius. On his way he had a vision, and according to the account of Lactantius, the contemporary Roman writer, "Constantine was directed in a dream to cause the 'heavenly sign' to be delineated on the shields of his soldiers, and so to proceed to battle."[2]

Constantine did as he had been commanded, and he replaced the imperial eagle on all the military standards with the monogram of Christ, the Greek letters X and P, the cipher we know today as the Chi Rho.

This gesture seems to have found favor with the soldiery, who had long since lost faith in the old pantheon of Roman gods in favor of a single God, for Constantine went on to win his battles. He became emperor, moved the imperial capital from Rome to Byzantium, and before he died, he adopted Christianity as the official religion of the empire. Perhaps Constantine's new standards were the first Christian banners!

You can see the Chi Rho monogram clearly on the shield held by the soldier on the left in figure 2. This mosaic, made in A.D. 547, comes from the church of San Vitale in Ravenna and shows one of Constantine's successors, Emperor Justinian-the-Great, with the Archbishop Maximinias of Ravenna bringing gifts to the altar. The insignia also appears in contemporary form on three altar frontals in the Danish, English, and United States sections of this book (see figs. 25b, 39b, 63).

THE EARLY CHURCH

Before Constantine, Christianity was an illicit religion that had been viciously persecuted by his predecessors, so that it had many of the attributes of a secret society. Its meetings took place in private houses, such as the house at Dura-Europos (modern Salhiyeh in Syria) illustrated in figure 3. This is thought to be the oldest-known church building still in existence. It was built as a private house in A.D. 232–233 and enlarged soon thereafter to accommodate a hundred people for worship.

1. Canadian liturgical artist Nancy-Lou Patterson was faced with the challenge of filling forty feet of space when she was asked to design a banner for St. Peter's Lutheran Church in Kitchener, Ontario, so patchwork seemed the obvious solution. Her impressive and colorful design is based on two crosses; one a living cross of green leaves with the dove of the Holy Spirit at its intersection, and the other an inverted cross, symbolizing the one on which St. Peter was martyred, with the words that Jesus said to him—"Feed My Sheep"—appliquéd on the crosspiece. Other images include the sun, the moon, and twelve stars. Nancy-Lou says, "When I presented the design, a slide of my rendering was projected onto the wall where the finished work was to go and I felt chills at seeing the image expanded to such a scale!" The finished banner is 29′ x 9′ (885 x 274 cm), the size of three queen-size quilts attached end-to-end, and it was pieced and quilted for her by Mennonite quilters in Ontario. (Photograph by Brian J. Thompson, Toronto, courtesy Helen Bradfield of Create & Celebrate Canada)

2. One of the oldest Christian insignia is the Chi Rho, the "heavenly sign" that Emperor Constantine saw in a vision in A.D. 312, and which he claimed God directed him to place on all military shields and standards. It is a monogram of the first two letters of Christ's name in Greek, X and P, and you can see it clearly on the shield carried by the soldier at the left. Constantine subsequently adopted Christianity as the official religion of the Roman Empire. The illustration also shows one of Constantine's successors, Emperor Justinian-the-Great, with the Archbishop of Ravenna, who is wearing the typical Roman clothing of the time from which our modern vestments derive: the long white robe known today as a dalmatic, the poncho-type cape called a *casula*, which became the chasuble, and a stole. Mosaic of A.D. 547 from San Vitale, Ravenna. (Photograph courtesy Fratelli Alinari I.D.E.A. S.p.A., Florence, Italy)

3. Before the time of Emperor Constantine, Christianity was an illicit religion and Christians met secretly in private houses. This photograph is of such a house in Dura-Europos (present-day Salhiyeh on the Euphrates River in Syria), and it is thought to be the oldest-known church building in existence today. It was built as a private house in A.D. 232–233, but one room was then enlarged to accommodate a hundred people for worship. The walls are decorated with scenes from the Old Testament and the Gospels. On the left you can see the baptistry in the northwest corner of the room—a large canopied bath with a pottery vessel on the side that held the Holy Water. Total submersion was the common form of baptism in those days. (Photograph courtesy Yale University Art Gallery, New Haven, Connecticut; Dura-Europos Collection)

The church used code words and symbols for recognition and identification of members, such as the fish and anchor you can see scratched on a fourth-century tombstone in the catacomb of St. Domitilla in Rome in figure 4. The anchor was, of course, a disguised cross that symbolized hope, while in the early days of Christianity, the fish was associated with baptism (little fish follow the Great Fish). Later on it became associated with the acrostic formed by the Greek word for fish (*ichthus*, meaning, in this context, "Jesus Christ, Son of God, Savior." The Christian community in Rome was Greek-speaking until the mid-third century.

Christians still use the fish today as a means of identification, often in the form of a lapel pin, and it is a popular motif for vestments, as you will see in the pages that follow.

Officials of the church wore ordinary civilian dress of the time, so they were indistinguishable from the man in the street. They wore a white full-length robe (an alb from the Latin word for white) and over it a cloak variously called a *casula* or *paenula* by the Romans, and before them a *phailones* by the Greeks. It was this word that St. Paul used when he wrote to Timothy: "When you come bring the cloak (*phailones*) that I left with Carpus at Troas... (2 Tim. 4:13 NIV). The modern chasuble takes its name and its form from the casula, which means "little house" or tent, and the cope from a bad-weather variation, a *pluvium* or rain cape with a hood that still survives on modern copes in a stylized form (see figs. 33, 65b, 99a, 100c).

They might also have worn a tunic-like garment that originated in Dalmatia and is called a *dalmatic* to this day. The archbishop's assistants in figure 2 are wearing dalmatics, as indeed is the archbishop himself under a dark green casula. Dalmatics are worn today by deacons in the Anglican and Roman Catholic churches, and also by British sovereigns during part of the Coronation Service.

The stole is also pre-Christian. In Roman times it was known as the *orarium* from the Latin word *oro* meaning "to pray," but originally it was a scarf worn by Roman officials as a sort of badge. The name was changed to *stola* in the ninth century (probably in Germany), and it is from this term that the modern English word "stole" derives. It is still a form of badge and is worn by bishops, priests, and deacons, each of whom wear it in a distinctive way.

After the accession of Emperor Constantine, the church came out in the open and public buildings were converted to use as meeting places. For example, the financial-market building in Ephesus became the church of St. Mary the Virgin, the ruins of which can still be seen at Ephesus in present-day Turkey. A dipping pool was usually constructed outside the church to baptize converts before they were admitted into the church, and it was only later that the baptistry was brought inside. Constantine himself had many church buildings constructed. Roman public buildings were known as basilicas, and comprised a hall (which subsequently became the nave) with a wing on each side (aisles), windows above (the clerestory), and a curved wall at the end known today as the apse. With modifications, churches maintained this structure for centuries.

Of course, not all denominations today use these ancient vestments, nor are modern churches necessarily built on traditional lines, yet it is astonishing to think that a priest wearing contemporary eucharistic vestments is dressed as he might have been in early Christian times. It can remind us that we are in touch with someone, who was in touch with someone, who was in touch with someone—who was in touch with Jesus Christ.

TIMES OF CHANGE

There have been, and continue to be, changes in church buildings and church vestments. In Byzantine times, bays were added to the standard basilica to give additional space for chapels. When the round Roman arches of these side bays (or transepts) met the nave at right angles, they were covered by the domed roof typical of Byzantine and Romanesque churches. In medieval times these transepts grew much bigger, and where the huge arches met at right angles to the nave, the structural problem was resolved by the invention of the pointed arch that gave birth to the magnificent lofty "Gothic" architecture of the twelfth century onward: the architecture of so many European cathedrals.

In the early days of the church in the western part of the Roman Empire, altars were placed at the western end of the church so that the rising sun shone toward the altar table. It was only in the eighth century that the position was reversed so that the light fell on the worshipers, as was the custom in the eastern part of the Empire. These may have been two different ways of looking at the same thing, namely the light of the world as a symbol for Jesus.

In those days, the priest faced the congregation, but in medieval times this changed. The priest became an intermediary, and the area of the altar assimilated to a "Holy of Holies." This was when the practice arose of screening off this area to form the chancel, or sanctuary, with the altar placed against the eastern wall, usually on a raised platform backed by a decorative screen, wall painting, carving, or sculpture known as the reredos.

In order to accommodate a number of officiating priests, the altar was elongated and then the ends were enclosed to create a tomb-shape that housed the holy relics venerated in medieval times.

The vestments of the clergy changed in sympathy. Since the priest now conducted the service facing the altar, with his back to the congregation, he needed to raise the host high over his head so that the congregation could see it. The ancient conical-shaped Roman cloak, the

4. These markings on an early fourth-century tomb in the catacombs of St. Domitilla in Rome are not as innocent as they seem. The person buried here belonged to a so-called "secret society" whose members had been subjected to vicious persecution by the Roman authorities. He or she was a Christian and this would have been evident to other Christians by the images of the fish and anchor. The anchor was, of course, a disguised cross symbolizing hope, while the fish was associated with the acrostic formed by the Greek word for fish (*ichthus*), meaning in this context "Jesus Christ, Son of God, Savior." In ancient Rome, the early Christians used the fish symbol as a means of identifying themselves. (Photograph courtesy Instituto Suore Benedittine di Priscilla, Rome)

5. In the Middle Ages, the position of the altar was changed, and this meant that the old Roman-style chasuble became impractical. Hitherto the priest had faced the congregation. Now he conducted the service facing the altar, with his back to the congregation, so that when the time came to show the host to the people, he was obliged to hold it high above his head so that they could see it. The heavy folds of the old conical-shaped chasuble were restrictive, so the sides were cut away and the vestment ceased to resemble the ancient Roman cloak. Here is an illustration of this cut-away Gothic style made in England in the early 1400s in red brocade that is charmingly patterned with marching camels. English embroidery of the Middle Ages was prized throughout Europe and was known as the Opus Anglicanum, or English work (see also fig. 7). The magnificently embroidered orphrey down the back is an example of this fine embroidery and shows the Crucifixion, and pairs of apostles and female saints, as well as the arms of the local benefactor of the church for which this chasuble was made, Sir Thomas Erpingham. A form of this cut-away Gothic style of chasuble is the one normally worn today, but now that church services have reverted to the ancient form where the priest once again faces the congregation, there is a revival of the original conical chasuble (see fig. 6). Erpingham Chasuble, England, fifteenth century. (Photograph courtesy the Trustees of the Victoria and Albert Museum, London)

chasuble, was all-enveloping, so the sides had to be cut away to give the priest freedom of movement. Chasubles became stiff ornate garments almost like tabards, narrow at the sides and often dropping to a point at the back and front. Some were even fashioned into a figure eight or were fiddle-shaped. A charming fifteenth-century example of this cut-away style in red brocade patterned with camels, called the Erpingham chasuble, is illustrated in figure 5. This change in shape and in ceremonial led to an increase in ornamentation.

However, now that church services are reverting to the ancient form where the priest once again faces the congregation, there is a revival of the ancient cloak, or conical-style chasuble of Roman times. A modern conical chasuble is illustrated in figure 6.

COMFORT FOR THE COLD

Some totally new garments made their appearance in the church wardrobe in the Middle Ages. In the cold northern churches it was customary to wear an undergown lined with fur, called a *pellicium*. Since it was difficult to don the narrow-sleeved alb over the fur garment, a wide-sleeved variety was adopted known as an "over-the-fur," a super-pellicium, or surplice as we know it today.

The cassock, the familiar black, long-sleeved, full-skirted clerical robe derives from medieval academic dress. In her book *Textile Art in the Church*, Marion P. Ireland says, "The rise of the universities, dating back to the twelfth century, occurred in a church-dominated society where most masters and scholars were in religious orders. A sober form of dress was worn as a uniform of sorts…and the loose cape and hood were worn as protection against the weather just as any citizen would wear. A gradual development led to the black robe and academic hood representing the degree and faculty that is now worn by ministers."[3] In 1604, it was decreed that the cassock should become the main outdoor garment of the clergy and it is worn during services by clergy of all denominations today, either under the alb and eucharistic vestments, or just with a stole.

The bishop's miter also took its modern form at this time, but it was not originally confined to bishops. It started life as a soft skullcap to cover the shaven head of a Roman man. In medieval times, the cap was looser fitting with ribbons or streamers at the back, and was pulled down lower on the head, resulting in folds at the sides. Later, the caps were stuffed to give them shape, and then some eccentric put the folded sides to the front and back and the folds became the twin peaks we know today. The streamers were retained as the lappets to be seen at the back of all modern miters.[4]

COLOR CODE

The medieval church authorities categorized a color code to be used at different seasons and for different ranks.

Such a code had existed in the Roman world, where different ranks of society wore different colors, with purple reserved exclusively for the emperor. Other Roman-rank colors were white, black, red, and gold—colors that were adopted by the early Christians and which are still used by churches today. You will find the sequence of liturgical colors used in Roman Catholic, Anglican, and Protestant churches in WAYS AND MEANS, section 3.

OPUS ANGLICANUM

The increase in display and ornamentation in the high medieval period reflected the wealth and power of the clergy. One of the glories of the time was embroidery, particularly embroidered work from England known as the Opus Anglicanum (English work). Since Saxon times in the ninth century, England had had a tradition of embroidery. Because it lay furthest away from the centers of silk weaving in Asia and Persia, the cost of importing silks with loom-woven patterns was extremely high, so decorating materials with embroidery became a special Anglo-Saxon skill. The bulk of the work in the high Middle Ages was produced in professional workshops, most of them in the city of London.

No English artistic product has ever achieved wider fame than the English work of the thirteenth and fourteenth centuries. The intricate and dazzling work has been likened to jewelry and was sought after by the popes and potentates of Europe. It was used in the ornamentation of contemporary liturgical vestments, and a beautiful example of late English work can be seen in figure 7.

This piece, known as the Syon Cope, was originally a chasuble that was converted into a cope at some point, and so it lost a fourth row of the embroidered quatrefoils, although some pieces of this missing fourth row were incorporated into the sides of the vestment during the remodeling. It belonged to an order of nuns from the Bridgettine Convent of Syon, a town just to the west of London that was founded in 1414, from which it takes its name.

The decline in English embroidery came as a result of the plague called the Black Death, which decimated Europe from the mid-1300s onward.

PATCHWORK TOO

Although many of these early embroidered vestments were cut down or remodeled (you will find many an old chasuble in museum collections with mismatched patterns and seams running at very odd angles—seen by candlelight such primitive patching did not show!), formal patchwork was also used by the church.

Such a piece is the fourteenth-century patchwork cope in figure 8 owned by Toledo Cathedral in Spain. This was made out of a royal mantle given to Don Sancho, Archbishop of Toledo, by the king of Aragon, who is known to have given many items of royal clothing to the cathedral, and it was probably made sometime during the 1300s. Don Sancho was the son of a former king of Aragon, James 1 (1208–1276). The cope is composed of octagons and squares embroidered with the coats of arms of the Spanish kingdoms of Aragon, Castile and Leon, and also the arms of Sicily, pieced together with squares of woven silk. It is usually on display in the Cathedral Treasury at Toledo.

There are few examples of medieval patchwork extant, but the practice of giving clothing and hangings to the church is well documented. In *Thread of Gold*, an account of the embroideries and textiles of York Minster edited by Elizabeth Ingram, Sylvia Hogarth says in the introductory essay, "Before the reformation it was the custom of every individual to bequeath a gift to the church…such gifts were known as mortuary gifts…in many places it was the tradition to give 'my best gown.'"[5]

Eleanor of Castile, wife of King Edward 1 of England, bequeathed her bed hangings to York Minster when she died in 1290. Queen Philippa of Hainault, wife of Edward III, gave a gift of bed hangings that were made into vestments in 1371 and which cost, according to the Minster records, £17/2s/11d to make up into "thirteen copes, six tunicles, and one chasuble."[6]

The custom of making vestments from clothing continued, and there is an example in York Minster of a dossal (an embroidered or decorated cloth that hangs behind the altar in place of a reredos), which was made in 1947 from the skirt of a magnificently embroidered ballgown dating from the mid to late 1730s (fig. 9).

In wartime Britain, when fine fabrics were unobtainable, many old dresses were recruited by the church and made into liturgical hangings.

Elizabeth Ingram also illustrates in her book another Low Mass set dated 1765–1770 which "has been re-made from a dress and signs of pleats remain from a sack-back."[7] A sack-back is a dress that has box pleats hanging from the neckline at the back.

REFORMATION

In the late 1400s, Martin Luther unleashed a movement of protest, the Reformation, against the church that resulted in a series of break-away Protestant churches throughout northern Europe. A common theme of the Protestant churches in their many denominations was revulsion against priestly intermediation and an emphasis upon salvation through individual faith. These ideas were reflected in the opening up of the chancel, the bringing of the altar (which now reverted to being just a table) into the body of the church, and adoption by the clergy, ministers, elders, or moderators of austere dress and of the way of life (including marriage) of laymen. Statues and images were removed, defaced, or destroyed as being "pagan," and decoration was frowned upon and removed.

The Roman Catholic church responded with a Counterreformation that emphasized an emotional and mystical appeal, which was reflected in elaborate ornamentation and in Baroque architecture. Elaborate vestments continued to be worn.

For more than one hundred years it was a time of mutual persecution between Roman Catholics and Protestants and their different denominations. An envoy from the Holy Roman Emperor Charles V, reported from London in 1529 that "nearly all the people here hate the priests."[8] Persecution of the Catholics was given additional impetus in England by Henry VIII's divorce from Catherine of Aragon in 1533, when he broke with Rome and forced his subjects to swear allegiance to himself as head of the church. Figure 10 shows a fascinating silk patchwork chasuble that possibly dates from this time, when Catholic priests were forced underground and many disguised themselves as peddlers, carrying their sacramental paraphernalia around in backpacks. The chasuble is believed to have been made by Elizabeth Belling Arundel about 1540 deliberately to resemble a domestic quilt so that if the priest were challenged, the chasuble would not attract attention. Many old mansions in England that belonged to Catholic families have hiding places known as "priest holes."

In England, by the end of the 1500s, only the cope (which was not regarded as a priestly or sacerdotal robe) and the surplice were in use—and the surplice was hotly contested. In many Protestant denominations the dress of the ministers was a simple version in black of the contemporary layman's wear—perhaps distinguished with a white collar or neck band. By the early 1800s, Jane Austen, the English novelist, comments that clergymen had begun to congratulate themselves that their dress was no different from that of "any gentleman."

LITURGICAL CHANGES

In the 1800s there was a swing back to ceremonial. In the Anglican church and other Protestant denominations, the medieval concepts of worship were revived, centering worship once again in the chancel before the high altar and with emphasis on the role of priests. The chasuble was reinstated and interest was renewed in the fabric and furniture of churches. There was a revival of Gothic architecture. A similar trend was apparent in the Roman Catholic church.

After World War I, the fashion changed direction again. The term *liturgy* comes from the Latin word *leiturgica*, meaning "the work of the people," and the Liturgical Movement aimed to bring back the practices of the early Christian churches, a fellowship of ordinary people with democratically appointed leaders. The movement

6. The shape of the chasuble remained virtually unchanged for approximately one thousand years and was a semicircle of fabric with the straight edges joined together down the front. During services, the priest was obliged to draw up some of the cloth at the sides in order to free his hands. This ancient style changed in the Middle Ages when the priest conducted the service facing the altar and a stiff tabard shape became fashionable (see fig. 5). Now that the liturgy is reverting to the earlier form, where the priest once again faces the congregation, there is a return to the old conical-shaped robe of Roman times. This fine example of a conical chasuble was made by a family firm of silk-weaving and vestment manufacturers in Wales, G.J. KilBride, and you can see from the rich folds across the front of the garment how much more of the fabric the priest must carry on his arms. Gilbert KilBride explains that in order to make such a chasuble practical for today, it is essential to use a pliable material with good draping qualities, and his firm weaves a superb product from spun silk. For more information about the KilBride fabrics please see WAYS AND MEANS, section 10. (Photograph courtesy G.J. KilBride, Abergavenny, Gwent, Wales)

7. Medieval English embroidery (known as the Opus Anglicanum, or English work) was one of the glories of the time and was collected by all European kings and potentates. Its genius lay in its richness and the way in which the professional embroiderers, most of them from the City of London, contoured their stitching to create wonderfully lifelike faces. A popular motif was the quatrefoil that was probably inspired by contemporary church architecture, notably the rose windows that are such a feature of the Gothic style. These quatrefoils were used to enclose scenes and figures, such as you see on this superb cope that belonged to an order of Catholic nuns from the Bridgettine Convent in Syon (a town just to the west of London), founded by King Henry V in 1414–1415. When England reverted to Protestantism at the beginning of the reign of Elizabeth I (1558–1603), the nuns were sent into exile and took the cope with them. After much wandering around Europe, the order finally settled in Portugal, where the cope remained until it was brought back to England around 1810. It is one of the masterpieces of the Opus Anglicanum and is known as the Syon Cope. (Photograph courtesy the Trustees of the Victoria and Albert Museum, London)

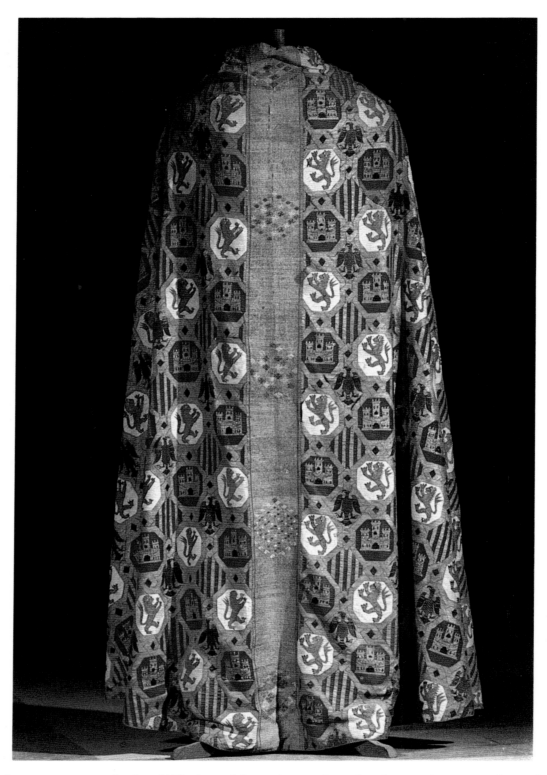

8. Patchwork is no newcomer to the church! This beautiful pieced cope is Spanish and was made sometime during the 1300s from a royal mantle given to Don Sancho, the Archbishop of Toledo, probably by the reigning king of Aragon who was known to have donated many such mantles to the cathedral in Toledo. Don Sancho himself was the son of a former king of Aragon, James I the Conqueror (1208–1276). The cope is composed of octagons and squares embroidered with the coats-of-arms of the kingdoms of Aragon, Castile and Leon, and also the arms of Sicily, together with squares of woven silk. It is described as "Don Sancho's chasuble" in the cathedral's English-language guidebook, but this is a mistranslation, for the Cathedral authorities confirmed that it is definitely a cope. It is usually on display in the Cathedral Treasury and is the oldest item in the cathedral's fine collection of embroideries. (Photograph courtesy the Holy Primate Cathedral, Toledo)

9. The custom of making vestments from items of clothing is well documented. The records of York Minster in England, for example, reveal it was the custom before the Reformation for ordinary people to give gifts of clothing to their local church, and in many cases this consisted of a "best gown." These were usually made into altar furnishings or vestments. This custom continued into this century, for in 1947 the regiment of the King's Own Yorkshire Light Infantry purchased a beautifully embroidered eighteenth-century ballgown to be made into a dossal (an embroidered or decorated cloth that hangs behind the altar in place of a reredos) for their chapel in York Minster to mark the visit of the regiment's Colonel-in-Chief, Her Majesty Queen Elizabeth, now the Queen Mother. On the right side of this detail taken from the dossal, you can see the scrolling acanthus leaves that originally formed the front edges of the skirt. The exquisite chinoiserie embroidery is contemporary with the dress, which was probably made during the 1730s. (Photograph by Jim Kershaw reproduced by kind permission of the Dean and Chapter of York)

10. Further proof that ornamental patchwork is no newcomer to the church is provided by this fascinating pieced-silk chasuble that is believed to have been made around 1540. During the Reformation, Roman Catholics were driven underground, and in England, persecution was given additional impetus by King Henry VIII's divorce from Catherine of Aragon in 1533, when he broke with Rome and forced his subjects to swear allegiance to himself as the head of the church. Recusant Catholic priests traveled to private houses to celebrate mass in peril of their lives, and many were forced to disguise themselves as peddlers, carrying their sacramental paraphernalia around in backpacks. Catholic families built hiding places in their mansions that are known today as "priest holes." The chasuble was probably deliberately made in patchwork so that if the priest were challenged, it could pass as a bedcover. For example, the clearly defined cross would probably have escaped detection when the garment was folded or rolled. The maker was Elizabeth Belling Arundel, a member of one of the leading Catholic families of England, and the chasuble has remained in the possession of the Arundel family from that time. (Photograph by Jim Pascoe reproduced by kind permission of Lord Talbot of Malahide)

11. Many familiar patchwork patterns have biblical names that were given to them by the pioneer women of America for whom the Good Book was a source of strength and solace. Every block in this attractive quilt, *Images of the Spirit* (1986), has a biblical reference. It was designed and pieced by Janet Aronson for a show organized by a group in Connecticut, the Parish Piecers (who did the quilting), to raise money for a new organ for Storrs Congregational Church. Starting from the top row left, and reading from left to right, the patterns are as follows: Walls of Jericho, Christian Cross, World Without End, King David's Crown, St. George's Cross, Tree of Paradise, Hosanna, Crown of Thorns, Caesar's Crown, Providence, David and Goliath, Job's Tears, Garden of Eden, Forbidden Fruit, Lily of the Field, Joseph's Coat, Devil's Claws, Jacob's Ladder, Cross and Crown, and Children of Israel. Having done its job of fund-raising, the quilt is now the property of May and Robert Guttay of Storrs, Connecticut. 96″ x 80″ (244 x 203 cm). (Photograph courtesy the artist)

The quilt patches contain the following hand-lettered biblical texts:

BEHOLD THE LAMB of GOD WHICH TAKETH AWAY THE SIN OF THE WORLD

THE BLOOD OF JESUS CHRIST HIS SON CLEANSETH US FROM ALL SIN.

THERE IS JOY IN THE PRESENCE OF THE ANGELS OF GOD OVER ONE SINNER THAT REPENTETH.

I AM THE GOOD SHEPHERD: THE GOOD SHEPHERD GIVETH HIS LIFE FOR THE SHEEP.

SEEK YE THE LORD WHILE HE MAY BE FOUND, CALL YE UPON HIM WHILE HE IS NEAR.

FOR THE WAGES OF SIN IS DEATH; BUT THE GIFT OF GOD IS ETERNAL LIFE THROUGH JESUS CHRIST OUR LORD.

BELIEVE ON THE LORD JESUS CHRIST AND THOU SHALT BE SAVED

BLESSED IS HE WHOSE TRANSGRESSION IS FORGIVEN, WHOSE SIN IS COVERED.

THERE REMAINETH THEREFORE A REST UNTO THE PEOPLE OF GOD.

12. Patches inscribed with hand-lettered biblical texts are a feature of this quilt top made in the late 1800s, when such stern exhortations were part of the fabric of daily life. Whether or not the maker bought these patches from a shop, or a catalog, or penned them herself is unclear. Their size is sufficiently uniform in comparison to the other charmingly patterned patches to suggest that this might well have been the case, but this appears to be the only biblical quilt in existence that has hand-lettered work of this nature. It would also be interesting to know why the quilt remained unfinished, since it might have served to strengthen the backbone of some half-hearted Christian had he, or she, slept under it night after night! 84″ x 106″ (213 x 269.7 cm). (Photograph courtesy Kelter-Malcé Antiques, New York)

continues to be influential to this day, with altars being brought forward into the nave in both Roman Catholic and Protestant churches and with the involvement of laymen in the conduct of worship services and the governance of the churches. The use of modern translations of the prayer books and Bibles and the abandonment of Latin in favor of the vernacular by the Roman Catholic church was part of this trend.

The decoration of the churches has also become the responsibility of the people and it is in this century, particularly since World War II, that patchwork has come into the church as an important decorative art, for vestments, hangings, altar frontals, dossals, pulpit falls, and all the other fabrics used in churches today.

OUTSIDE THE CHURCHES

It is not only within the churches that patchwork is an expression of Christian faith. Religion was the inspiration of our forbears in their daily lives. In the United States, the pre-eminent home of patchwork, many of the patterns developed during Victorian times have biblical names, as illustrated in Janet Aronson's sampler quilt *Images of the Spirit* in figure 11. It is not always easy for the modern eye to discern the connection between the block and its name, but for our ancestors the natural description of a form was in biblical terms. The Bible was part of the texture of life, and the quilt top shown in figure 12, with its patches of hand-lettered texts, breaks into the type of exhortation that was common in the Victorian era. No doubt such a quilt lit the way for many a questing soul!

Religion also dominated the lives of the Amish people and in their book *A Gallery of Amish Quilts* Robert Bishop and Elizabeth Safanda suggest that the familiar design of a Center Diamond of the early Amish quilts (fig. 13) may have been inspired by the outer leather bindings of their family hymnals known as *Ausbunds* (fig. 14)[9]. Amish women did not have access to popular books and magazines that featured quilt patterns (these appeared as early as 1840), nor were they surrounded by fancy textiles or wallpapers in their austere homes. But the hymnal was always to hand and this became their matrix, not only in their lives but in their quiltmaking.

Making quilts to raise funds was a popular cooperative church activity. A well-known design in the last century was the one shown on the quilt in figure 15, which was made by members of a Methodist church in Ohio to raise money. The names of sponsors were stitched on the quilt for twenty-five cents each. The quilt probably dates from the latter half of the last century. Interestingly, the design crossed the Atlantic because there is a similar quilt in England owned by the Bar Methodist Chapel in Harrogate, Yorkshire, which was made in 1889 and raised the princely sum (in those days) of £50 (fig. 16). Many more quilts of a similar design exist in the United States

and in the Doon Heritage Crossroads collection in Kitchener, Ontario, Canada.

MISSIONARY ACTIVITY

Patchwork was a missionary activity in the evangelization of the Hawaiian Islands, among other places. New England Protestant missionaries taught patchwork to Hawaiian womenfolk as a useful occupation to counter their apparently feckless way of life. Joyce D. Hammond in *Tīfaifai and Quilts of Polynesia* says that they probably started with "women of the royal households as a strategy to influence the general population."[10] The Polynesians took to the art with enthusiasm, and although they quickly elaborated the craft with their own lexicon of exotic appliqué patterns, it was actually piecework that they learned from the missionaries. An example of pieced Hawaiian quilts being used in unusual circumstances is shown in figure 17, where the quilts are used as floor coverings in Our Lady of Peace Cathedral in Honolulu during the High Mass held to commemorate the death of King Alphonso of Spain in January 1866.

ARTISTS IN THE CHURCH

Finally, we must not forget the contribution made by artists to the church. The tradition is as old as the church itself, for the highest achievement of a work of art is to glorify God.

During the Renaissance all artists worked for the church, Michelangelo being the most obvious example. In our own time, we have the work of the world-famous French painter, Henri Matisse (1869–1954), who not only designed the Chapel of the Rosary in Vence, France, to be a "religious space" to be decorated with his paintings, but also designed sets of vestments that would echo and repeat the colors and motifs that appear in his exquisite stained-glass windows (figs. 18a, 18b).

A number of these sets of eucharistic vestments are now owned by The Museum of Modern Art in New York, and one of Matisse's chasubles is shown in figure 18c. Floral motifs in their various forms are a feature of many Matisse's paintings, but he also used them on the walls and in the stained-glass windows of the chapel. Matisse worked out all his designs in gouache and paper, and the edges of the stitched silk appliqués on the chasuble retain the same uneven contours of his original maquettes.

The various parts of the church, the origin of vestments, historical changes, and spiritual concepts can all give rise to appropriate decorative themes. In the following sections of this book you can see for yourself how quilt-makers from all over the world have drawn on these sources to produce work that expresses the liturgy through their hands.

ANDREW LIDDELL

13. This striking woolen Amish quilt from Lancaster County, Pennsylvania, was made around 1920, and it shows how the Amish quilters found inspiration for their designs in religious objects in their homes. The classic design of a Center Diamond, flanked by smaller squares in each corner, could well have been copied from their leather-bound hymnals (see fig. 14). 77″ x 77½″ (196 x 197 cm). (Photograph courtesy Thos. K. Woodard: American Antiques & Quilts, New York)

14. According to Robert Bishop and Elizabeth Safanda in their book *A Gallery of Amish Quilts* (1976), Amish families often passed their family hymnals (known as *Ausbunds*) down through the generations, and the authors were struck by the way that the shape and placement of the brass bosses almost exactly resembles the basic design of a pieced Amish quilt (see fig. 13). In the above illustration, the center hymnal, printed in 1801, is probably the most illustrative of this type of design. Here you can see a center diamond flanked by four corner squares. The authors also note that the scroll designs blind-tooled on the leather bindings are similar to the elegant stitching found on the borders of Amish quilts even today. (Photograph courtesy Museum of American Folk Art, New York)

15. Making and selling, or raffling quilts to raise funds for churches has probably been a popular occupation for American women ever since quilts first began to be made, but in the latter half of the last century, a different type of fund-raising quilt began to emerge. This daisy-wheel design is a typical example. It was made by members of a Methodist Church in Ohio, and here the names of sponsors were embroidered on the spokes for the sum of twenty-five cents each. The quilt was presented to the minister, Charles H. Stocking, who was born in 1842. There are many quilts of a similar nature still to be found in the United States and Canada, and interestingly, the design also crossed the Atlantic (see fig. 16). (Photograph courtesy Smithsonian Institution, Washington D.C.)

16. Here is a transatlantic cousin of the quilt shown in figure 15. This detail of a daisy-wheel quilt embroidered with sponsors' names comes from a fund-raising quilt that was made in England. It is owned by the Bar Methodist Church (known locally as Bar Chapel) in Harrogate, Yorkshire, who say that it was made in order to raise funds to help pay off the cost of building the church, which was opened in 1889. There are 1038 names embroidered on the quilt and the project realized £50. A present-day member of the congregation, Dorothy Fieldhouse, who is aged seventy-three, says she can remember that in her childhood tablecloths were also embroidered with sponsors' names to raise funds. (Photograph courtesy P.V.C. Manning, L.R.P.S., Harrogate)

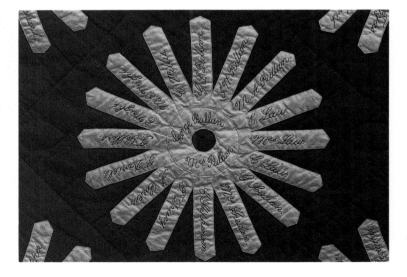

17. Patchwork was also a missionary activity in Polynesia among other places, particularly in the Hawaiian islands where it was taught as a useful occupation and to counter the seemingly feckless way of life of Hawaiian women. That quiltmaking was one of the more successful transplants is apparent in the magnificent Hawaiian appliqué designs that are admired today all over the world. What is less well known is that it was piecework that was commonly used in the early days, and that the name all Polynesians use for their quilts, *tīfaifai*, means literally "to patch repeatedly." Quilts are used as decoration throughout Polynesia, particularly for solemn or social occasions. They are displayed on the walls, on tables, or even as floor-coverings such as you see here. This photograph shows how the Hawaiians placed pieced quilts on the floor of Our Lady of Peace Cathedral in Honolulu for the High Mass that was held to commemorate the death of King Alphonso of Spain in January 1866. (Photograph courtesy the Bishop Museum, Honolulu)

18a, 18b, and 18c. The highest achievement of art is to glorify God, and the church has been the patron of artists since its foundation. In our own time, we have the work of the French painter Henri Matisse (1869–1954) who, in the 1920s, designed and decorated the Chapel of the Rosary in Vence, France, as a "religious space" (fig. 18a). The joy that Matisse took in creating pure shape and color through the medium of his cutouts, which blossomed toward the end of his career, is evident in the decoration of this chapel. The blossom motifs in the stained-glass windows shown in figure 18b illustrate his delightful inventiveness, and you can see that he used a variation of this blossom motif on the chasuble in figure 18c. Matisse liked to work out his designs in paper, and the edges of the stitched-silk appliqués retain the same uneven contours of his original maquettes. Several of these sets of vestments are now owned by The Museum of Modern Art in New York. Silk chasuble with silk appliqués. 52⅛″ x 73¾″ (132.4 x 187.4 cm). Manufactured by Atelier d'Arts Appliqués, Cannes, France. The Museum of Modern Art, New York; Gift of Mrs. Gertrud A. Mellon; © 1993 Succession H. Matisse/ARS, New York. (Photograph of the Chapel of the Rosary courtesy the Chapel)

A Pilgrim's Guide to Europe: Denmark, Sweden, England, and France

Every generation has its own interpretation of the Bible and its own way of expressing that interpretation in architecture, art, ceremonial, decoration, and vestments. Each country adds its own nuance to that expression, so that in the continent of Europe, with its long history and many nationalities, there is a diversity spread over time and space. But within that diversity there are certain discernible rhythms.

For example, as Europe emerged from the Dark Ages, the church was a missionary organization. Brave priests like Saint Augustine in England, Saint Columbanus in Burgundy, Saint Gall in Suabia, and Saint Boniface in Germany, went into barbarian territory to evangelize the heathen. Churches were simple structures. The priests would put a roof over the altar, and the congregation would build the nave with their own hands. It was a do-it-yourself church and the structures were solid, simple, and bare. But in southern and eastern Europe, still under the influence of Byzantium, there remained a rich decorative tradition with wonderful mosaics and icons.

As mentioned in the introduction, the high-medieval period interpreted the Bible through the clergy. This seemed quite natural, because learning and scholarship were confined to the clergy and they saw their role as mediators between God and man, rather on the lines of the Jewish priesthood. In northern Europe, this was expressed in pinnacled Gothic architecture such as the magnificent Salisbury Cathedral in Wiltshire, England (figs. 19, 20).

Southern Europe, however, retained the Romanesque styles. Indeed, the word Gothic was a term of contempt of what was perceived by the sophisticated southerners as a barbarian style.

Decoration flourished with marvelous painted interiors, and richly embroidered fabrics, notably the *Opus Anglicanum* from England (see figs. 5, 7) and loom-woven brocaded fabrics from the more industrialized south.

As learning spread more widely through the lay world, interpretations of the Bible proliferated. The Reformation ushered in by Martin Luther looked back to Saint Paul, the doctrine of justification by faith and the do-it-yourself Christianity of the earlier days. Protestantism splintered into different denominations with many shades of faith. Individualism was encouraged and secularization followed—*cujus regio, ejus religio* (whoever governs decides the religious practice)!

An English appliqué altar frontal of the mid-1500s nicely illustrates this attitude (fig. 21). The central figure of Jesus on the Cross, with St. John and the Virgin Mary on either side, is not surrounded by other apostles, saints, or martyrs but by the Earl of Westmoreland and his family. The earl, seen with his seven sons on the left, probably owned the living and the church for which the frontal was made. On the right kneels the countess and behind her their thirteen daughters. (Lady Westmoreland was surely something of a martyr!) It is a marvelous piece of work

and one of the earliest examples of the use of appliqué in church decoration.

In southern Europe a different spirit prevailed. The Counterreformation of the Roman Catholic church inspired a spirit of romantic mysticism and produced the marvelously colorful buildings in the Baroque style, with barley sugar pillars, huge paintings, reredos like opera settings, and lavish draperies (fig. 22). But in northern Europe the Baroque movement was much more austere: German churches with onion domes painted yellow and the clean lines of Saint Petersburg. Vestments were those of a civilian schoolmaster in black.

In the 1700s, the churches became more worldly and skeptical, but the seeds of a new spirituality emerged with Charles Wesley and the Methodist movement in northern Europe, and a puritanism with the Jansenist movement in the Roman Catholic church.

The rhythm changed again in the 1800s, when there was a revival of the concept of priestly intermediation, both in the various Protestant and Roman Catholic churches. A new scholarship and interest in research permeated the clergy. Vestments and ceremonial were reintroduced in many Protestant churches that formerly had shunned them; the chancel and the high altar became the focus of worship again. In architecture the Gothic style was reintroduced.

The spirit of the period can be seen in the fascinating mosaic patchwork in figure 23. This was made in 1876 by an old English lady called Miss Hepzibah Harris who lived in a cottage in Stratford-upon-Avon, not far from the Shakespeare Memorial Theatre. She delighted in making patchwork pictures that she exhibited in her living room and charged visitors an entrance fee of one penny to see. It shows a christening taking place in the baptistry of Holy Trinity church in Stratford-upon-Avon. This picture, and three more examples of Miss Harris's work, hang in the theater restaurant today, two of them depicting other scenes in the church.

In this century, emphasis has changed again toward the simplicity of the early church. The altar has moved back into the nave, and lay people have become more involved in the decoration of their churches. Patchwork and appliqué have a special role to play because of their ability to cover large areas and create beautiful effects comparatively economically in terms of time and cost.

In interpreting the Bible, the rhythms will continue to oscillate. Since the Reformation, there has continued to be proliferation in the ways of worshiping. The opening up of the United States of America and other new continents and countries has accelerated the creation of new churches. Some people may regret these divisions, but kaleidoscopic human nature demands that each one of us must find a way to express faith individually, and the unity of the church must be that we all hold fast to Christ and, for the rest, accept our differences.

ANDREW LIDDELL

19. "The whole pile is large and magnificent and may be justly accounted one of the best patterns of architecture in that age wherein it was built." So wrote the famous British architect Sir Christopher Wren, after he had inspected Salisbury Cathedral in 1689. Salisbury Cathedral, one of England's finest Gothic buildings, is a perfect example of the Gothic style because there were no changes in the original architectural design during the construction and no long periods when work stopped. Nor have there been any major alterations or additions since. The cathedral was built in the shape of a cross and was completed in one continuous operation beginning in 1220, when the foundation stone was laid, to the finishing of the spire about a hundred years later. The surroundings add considerably to its beauty, for the cathedral is set in a large grassy area surrounded by a Close containing many seventeenth-century houses and the Bishop's Palace, which now houses the Cathedral School. The school was founded in 1091 elsewhere in the Close, and in figure 20 you can see an altar frontal made by the children to celebrate its 900th anniversary. The cathedral authorities have also commissioned some fine modern altar furnishings and vestments and these appear further on in figures 35 and 36. (Photograph courtesy Pitkin Pictorials, Andover, England)

20. The Cathedral School in Salisbury is now housed in the old Bishop's Palace that stands in the shadow of the magnificent cathedral (fig. 19), and this is where many of the choristers are educated. To mark the 900th anniversary of the foundation of the school, the "Friends of the School" decided to give to the chapel a new altar frontal that could be made by the children themselves. They asked Jane Lemon, a leading British liturgical artist who has designed many pieces for the cathedral (see figs. 35, 36), to help them and, realizing that she was limited by what the children could manage, Jane designed a rainbow of hexagons arching over the cathedral spire. The crowning glory of Salisbury is the spire that has been a landmark for pilgrims since the fourteenth century. Heather Scutt, the project organizer, assembled a team of keen (and not so keen!) boys and girls and three mothers. The frontal, beautifully worked in colored silks on a cotton background, took six months to make and during that time, even the unwilling members of the team were converted. When the dedication service took place on July 3, 1991, excitement was intense throughout the school. The lettering worked in gold leather is the school motto. (Photograph by PhotoShades, Salisbury, England, reproduced by kind permission of the Cathedral School)

21. Individualism in the church flourished after the Reformation, and a secular influence became noticeable. The profusion of saints and martyrs that were such a feature of the embroidered church furnishings of the Opus Anglicanum do not appear on this sixteenth-century altar frontal. Instead, we see the patron of the church for which the frontal was made, the fourth Earl of Westmoreland and his family flanking the figure of Christ on the Cross. The earl in full armor and surcoat kneels at the left with his seven sons behind him, while on the right is his wife with their thirteen daughters. (After bearing twenty children, Lady Westmoreland surely deserved to be either a saint or a martyr!) Above their heads are the heraldic shields of both their families. It is a delightful frontal for all its worldly appearance, and it is an early example of appliqué in church decoration. The two figures on each side of Our Lord are St. John and the Virgin Mary. (Photograph courtesy the Trustees of the Victoria and Albert Museum, London)

22. The southern Baroque style of architecture was one of sensuous theatricality and lavish decoration, designed to appeal to the emotions rather than to reason, and was in direct contrast to the classical style that preceded it. This superb high altar can be seen in the pilgrimage church of the Vierzehnheiligen (meaning "fourteen saints") near Bamberg in Bavaria, which was built in 1700–1743 by the architect Johann Balthasar Neumann, one of the greatest architects of the eighteenth century. (Photograph courtesy John Jeffery, London)

23. This charming scene of a Christmas baptism (the church is hung with Christmas decorations) was made in 1876 by an old English lady called Miss Hepzibah Harris who lived in the center of Stratford-upon-Avon, around the corner from the Shakespeare Memorial Theatre. She delighted in making patchwork mosaics of scenes in Stratford that she used to exhibit in her living room and charge the public an entrance fee of one penny to see. A visitor remembers Miss Harris in 1912 as being "a very spry little woman with bright black eyes."[11] The figures gathered around the font are superbly dressed in wool, tweed, and velvet while the baby's christening robe is made of *broderie anglaise*. The beautifully worked stained-glass window and the architecture are faithful representations of Holy Trinity Church in Stratford, where Shakespeare was baptized on April 26, 1564. Miss Harris left her fascinating pictures to the Shakespeare Memorial Theatre, and this particular mosaic can be seen, together with three others, in the theater restaurant. Sixteen more hang in the theater itself. 32″ x 21¼″ (81 x 54 cm). (Photograph courtesy the RSC Collection, with the permission of the Governors of the Royal Shakespeare Theatre, Stratford-upon-Avon, England)

Denmark and Sweden

We begin our European pilgrimage in Denmark where patchwork has acquired a royal seal of approval! Her Majesty, Queen Margrethe II of Denmark, a talented artist in her own right, has used piecework in many of her designs for church textiles over the years. You can see the evidence in figures 24, 25a, 25b, 26a, 26b, 26c, 27a, and 27b.

The Queen's diverse talents are not solely confined to church work. In spite of her many official duties, she has also undertaken commissions to design postage stamps, costumes for Danish Television, embroideries, enamel work, and book illustrations. Her drawings, published under the pseudonym Ingahild Grathmer, were used in the illustrated edition of Tolkien's *Lord of the Rings* published by the Folio Society, London, in 1977.

In 1988, an exhibition of the Queen's work (all of it commissions of one sort or another) was held in Køge to celebrate the town's 700th jubilee, and in the foreword to the catalogue of the exhibition the Queen confesses that although she always loved to draw as a child, she could not stand needlework. She says that "the idea of sewing neat stitches...not to mention threading a needle!" was anathema to her, but one day she saw her mother's big bundle of colored cotton yarn "in all the delightful colors of the Danish Handcraft Guild and I began to embroider."[12] She adds that the interplay of stitch, fabric, and color "...present a frame to be accomplished, while at the same time holding one in check. I think it gave me the discipline that I needed."[13]

In 1976, the Queen designed three chasubles for Fredensborg Palace church (the Queen's summer palace in Helsingor) on the occasion of its 250th anniversary. One of them, a violet chasuble worn during Lent, had a patchwork cross on the back that was pieced in small squares by her sister, Her Royal Highness Princess Benedikte, with pieces from the royal scrapbag, including pieces from the dresses worn by the young princesses at their confirmation. In 1985, the Queen chose to use patchwork again for the stunning chasuble for Angmagssalik church in Greenland, which you can see in figures 27a and 27b. This was also worked by Princess Benedikte.

That same year, the parochial church council of Haderslev Cathedral in South Jutland decided to renovate the cathedral's interior and asked the Queen if she would be prepared to design four sets of furnishings in brilliant liturgical colors to enhance the simple white Gothic nave (fig. 24). The Queen became the artistic driving force behind the project, which must be one of the most comprehensive undertaken by a Danish church. Between 1985 and 1987, she paid seventeen visits to the cathedral to discuss her designs and to see whether or not the fabrics she had chosen created the right effect. Proof, if any were needed, of the care and dedication that Queen Margrethe brings to all her work.

The fabrics for two of the sets were woven by Danish weavers, but the Queen herself provided many of the fabrics for the two pieced and machine-appliqué sets seen in figures 25a, 25b, 26a, 26b, 26c. These included beautiful pieces of silk and brocade that she had collected during her official visits to China, Japan, India, and Egypt. Some also came from Fredensborg Palace and dated from her great-grandmother's time.

When speaking of her work, Queen Margrethe says that in the final analysis it is subjects with predefined limits that inspire her most. "There is a special challenge in creating something to be used in a particular way and in a particular place. In the case of church fabrics there is a rich tradition on which to build....It is necessary to try to interact with what already exists and at the same time to subordinate oneself to something in every way greater than oneself."[14]

The Queen's words would no doubt be echoed by all the other talented needlewomen whose work you will see as we continue on our pilgrimage around the world.

ANDREW LIDDELL

24. The interior of Haderslev Cathedral in South Jutland, Denmark. The green altar frontal was designed by Queen Margrethe II. It is one of a set of four that the Queen designed for the cathedral between 1985–1987, two of which are woven and two are pieced. This is one of the designs woven by Ann-Mari Kornerup. The pieced vestments appear in figures 25b and 26b and 26c. (Photograph courtesy Jørgen Grønlund, Allerød, Denmark)

25a, 25b. *Festal Chasuble and Altar Frontal* designed by Queen Margrethe II for Haderslev Cathedral, South Jutland, Denmark. 1987. Sewing and mounting by Ulla Esholdt Olsen and Vibeke Blach Nielsen of the Society of Ecclesiastical Art, Copenhagen, under the direction of Lillian Damgaard Christiansen. Silk brocade, shantung lining. Machine-piecing and appliqué. White is the liturgical color of celebration, and white vestments are used on all feast days such as Christmas, Easter, and All-Saints Day, but because Haderslev Cathedral's nave is white (see fig. 24) the Queen decided to add bright golds and yellows to her design. She also selected pieces of rich brocade to emphasize the festive feeling. Some were antique and came from Fredensborg (the Queen's summer palace), and some were new and came from China, Japan, or India. The center of the frontal is dominated by a pieced sun (fig. 25a) that is set within a haloed cross taken from an old Celtic design. In her book, *The Queen's Work of Art in Haderslev Cathedral*, Søren Lodberg Hvas says that "... the beams of light continue to the edge of the communion table... as a reminder of the radiance which disperses from the news of Christ who has conquered death and darkness."[15] The Queen's design for the beautiful chasuble in figure 25b continues this theme inasmuch as the simple appliqué cross on the back is barely visible against the radiance of the vertical rays of light. (Photographs by Jørgen Grønlund, Allerød, Denmark, reproduced by gracious permission of Her Majesty Queen Margrethe II of Denmark)

26a, 26b, 26c. *Red Altar Frontal and Chasuble* designed by Queen Margrethe II for Haderslev Cathedral, South Jutland, Denmark. 1987. Piecework by Ellen Kragh Mortensen, Vojens. Silver and gilded, hammered-brass plates by silversmith Erik Sjødahl, Copenhagen. Mounting by Jytte Harboesgaard and Vibeke Vlach Nielsen of the Society of Ecclesiastical Art, Copenhagen, under the direction of Lillian Damgaard Christiansen. Silks, gilded leather, shantung lining. Hand-piecing over cardboard. When the Queen undertook the commission for Haderslev Cathedral, she wanted local people to be involved, and Ellen Kragh Mortensen, a housewife and skilled quiltmaker, was honored to be one of those who were asked. The cross is the unifying symbol. On the altar frontal (fig. 26a) small pieced crosses are set within a larger cross surrounded by hammered-brass plates. A pieced cross is repeated again on the front of the chasuble (fig. 26b) while for the back (fig. 26c) the queen designed a stylized form of the ancient Chi Rho symbol (see fig. 2). This is the "heavenly sign," the monogram for Christ that the Emperor Constantine saw in a vision in the year A.D. 312, and which he had placed on all his military equipment. The Queen also included on the back of the chasuble the first and last letters of the Greek alphabet, Alpha and Omega. They refer to the passage in Revelations 1:8 (NIV) "I am the Alpha and the Omega," said the Lord God, "who is, and who was, and who is to come, the Almighty." Sadly, this magnificent set of vestments is only used at Pentecost, All Saints' Day, and on St. Stephen's Day (the day after Christmas), which led the Queen to explain at the press conference held at the time of the consecration that this was the reason why she had used strong colors. ". . . And if anybody in the parish thinks that it is too much, he or she can look forward to not seeing it again too soon!"[16] (Photographs by Jørgen Grønlund, Allerød, Denmark, reproduced by gracious permission of Her Majesty Queen Margrethe II of Denmark)

27a, 27b. *Chasuble* designed by Queen Margrethe II for Angmagssalik Church, Greenland. 1985. Hand-pieced by Princess Benedikte, gold-thread embroidery by Lillian Damgaard Christiansen, mounting by Ulla Esholdt Olsen and Lillian Damgaard Christiansen of the Society of Ecclesiastical Art, Copenhagen. Shantung, Thai silks. The royal sisters have been interested in patchwork for many years and it is believed that the inspiration came originally from their mother, Queen Ingrid, who is also a needlewoman of note. Greenland is part of the kingdom of Denmark (it sends representatives to the Danish parliament), and when the church at Angmagssalik was built, knowing of the Queen's interest in church furnishings, the church authorities asked her if she would consider designing a special chasuble to be worn at the inauguration in 1985. You can see the finished piece worn by the priest, Aaron Davidsen, in figure 27a. It is believed that the beautiful design of radiant circles reflects the same theme of "light in the dark" that the Queen used for a Christmas postage stamp she had designed for Greenland in 1983. Because of its proximity to the Arctic circle, there is very little light in Greenland during the winter, and on the back of the chasuble some of the circles contain a golden flame (fig. 27b). The beautiful colors of the circles may have been inspired by the *aurora borealis* (the northern lights), which are such a feature of the Arctic summer. Notice that on the front of the chasuble the Queen has included in her design a fish, an ancient symbol of Christianity (see fig. 4). Princess Benedikte, who did all the piecing, was invited to the inauguration ceremony and traveled to Greenland with the architect, Jørgen Glahn, but unfortunately bad weather prevented them from reaching Angmassalik. They spent three days marooned in the capital before returning to Denmark. (Photographs by Arne R. Olsen, Angmagssalik, Greenland, reproduced by gracious permission of Queen Margrethe II of Denmark)

28a, 28b. *Purple Chasuble* designed by Mana Torne, Gilleleje, Denmark, for Gilleleje Church, assisted by Connie Holm Jensen, Anni Neertoft, Elsa Kejlbo, and Aase Lund. 1990. Silk, cotton poplin, gray silk from old ties.

White Chasuble designed by Mana Torne for Blistrup Church, North Sjælland, Denmark, assisted by Edith Barkley Jensen, Marie Andersen, Gerda Kristiansen, Rigmor Larsen, and Hanne Borello. Wild silk, cotton satin, poplin. Both chasubles hand-pieced over cardboard, hand-quilted.

Mana Torne trained as a fashion designer and these two superb chasubles are her first attempt at church work ("but not, I hope, the last!"). She was asked by some students from her patchwork classes if she would design a purple chasuble for them to make for Gilleleje Church because the church did not have one. The idea of a group project in piecework appealed to her for several reasons. "Most of the world's religions use geometric patterns for decoration and as symbolic imagery," she explains. "The crusaders used patchwork for their banners and horse-trappings, but also, women have traditionally used their sewing skills to contribute to the decoration and comfort of their churches. This created a bond between the church and the people which is in danger of being lost today because so many church textiles are bought ready-made. I felt that the tranquil and meditative atmosphere that arises from this kind of communal activity harmonizes very well with the ideals of the church."

The symbolism behind the two designs is fascinating. For the purple chasuble, Mana chose the hexagon, "a symbol of rebirth and resurrection," and by placing equilateral triangles (itself a symbol of the Holy Trinity) around the sides, she created the Jewish emblem, the Star of David. During World War II, many Danish Jews took refuge in Gilleleje Church before fleeing to Sweden in local fishing boats and Mana commemorates the fact that Gilleleje is a fishing village by including two fish on the back of the robe (fig. 28b). The fish is also an ancient symbol for Christianity.

The white chasuble was also a group project and was commissioned by the women of nearby Blistrup Church after they had heard about the purple chasuble. The gold cross on the back of the white chasuble represents stalks of wheat, for Blistrup Church is at the heart of a farming community and wheat is a symbol of the Eucharist. (The Virgin Mary is often depicted with a stalk of wheat in her hand as a sign of blessing.) At the hem of the robe, the wheat cross is seen growing out of a stylized mound, which is an allusion to Blistrup's hilly terrain and to the numerous Nordic burial mounds, and to Golgotha itself. In the photographs the ministers of both churches are wearing their respective vestments. The unusual tabard-shape of the vestments comes from a sixteenth-century Norwegian chasuble. (Photographs courtesy Jens Bull)

29a, 29b. *Altar Frontlet* designed by Kirsten Dissing Overgaard and Aase Pedersen for Bering Free Church, Bering, Denmark, and made by Anna Kristensen, Martha Kristensen, Ruth Jensen, Anna Bent Andersen, Elna Lildholdt, and Herdis Fogh. 1987. 8″ x 132″ (21 x 336 cm). Handspun linen, cottons. Hand-pieced and quilted with gold thread. This enchanting frontlet was made by a group who belong to a free church formed in the last century, whose followers are known as "the merry Christians." It was the inspiration of the minister, Kirsten Dissing Overgaard. In 1986, knowing that Aase Pedersen, a member of the congregation, taught patchwork, Kirsten asked a group of ladies if they would be prepared to make a pieced altar frontal for the church. The ladies were reluctant at first, uncertain whether or not such an unusual form of needlework would be acceptable to other members of the congregation, but they are not called "merry Christians" for nothing! Kirsten drew the design, Aase made the templates, and Herdis dyed some of the fabrics, which included some fine handspun linen left to the church by an elderly member of the congregation. The frontlet was finished in 1987 and the congregation loved it. It is used at Advent, Christmas, Easter, and Pentecost. The rosettes represent the Christmas rose and daffodils, seasonal flowers that are used as symbols for Christ in old Danish hymns. The group so enjoyed the experience that they then made two fund-raising quilts and a second frontlet for the summer. (Photographs courtesy Herdis Fogh)

30a, 30b. *Log Cabin Chasuble* made by Tove Basse Tuiskoer, Fredericia, Denmark, for Smidstrup Church. 1987. Raw silk, Thai silk, linen, viscose, synthetics. Machine-pieced and quilted. Here the familiar Log Cabin style of quilting takes on a new form as a beautifully worked chasuble. It was made by Tove Basse for the pastor at her local church, and since then she has made two others. Tove explains the symbolism of the piece: "From my childhood I have collected samples of golden fabrics such as brocade and fine leather (my family owned a factory making evening bags). These pieces helped to formulate my design but I had many sleepless nights before it all came together! The small, self-colored cross at the lower edge on the front symbolizes the church that is all around us in everyday life but is invisible (fig. 30a), while the other Log Cabin blocks represent the congregation, same in form but different in substance. No human beings are alike, so none of my blocks are alike, and each one contains a small piece of gold that represents God. One color taken from either of the two crosses is also present in each block as a symbol of the small part of Christ that became mankind." The shimmering fabrics enhance the spirituality of this interesting piece, and Tove says that she made it heart-shaped "because love is the greatest gift of all." (Photographs courtesy the artist)

31a, 31b, 31c, 31d. *Ølsemagle Church Quilt*, Koge, Denmark, designed by Nina Christensen Ulriksen and made by Britta Jensen, Inger Bonde, Tove Folkmann, Birgit Hansen, Aase Hemmingsen, Anita Jacobsen, Iris Jacobsen, Malene Jacobsen, Grethe Koue, Ellen Lynge, Anni Gram Petersen, Alice Rasmussen, Yvonne Villumsen. 1990. 74″ x 89″ (187 x 225 cm). Cottons, chintz. Hand-pieced, appliqué, quilted, and embroidered. This charming group quilt acts as a link between the old village church in Ølsemagle and the parish hall that became separated from it by a highway and the suburban railroad tracks during the postwar expansion of Copenhagen. The parish hall is the workplace of the church—the minister has his office there and it is where all parish meetings are held. The congregation found the separation distressing, and the noise from the highway made it impossible even to hear the church bells ringing, so a group decided to make a quilt that would "bring the church to the parish hall." Nina and Britta decided to include some of the architectural features from both the outside and inside of the church, which appear in the detail photographs of the painted flowers on the sides of the pews and the gabled pew ends. The quilt was consecrated at the Harvest Festival in 1990 and then was taken to be hung in the parish hall, where the quilters' husbands had prepared a celebration supper. Not only did the men cook the food, they also serenaded the quilters with a song about the project! (Photographs courtesy Nina Christensen Ulriksen)

32. *Himlaljus* (*Light of Heaven*) designed by Gunvor Lindroos, Stockholm, Sweden, for Tacksägelsekyrkan, Karlsborg. 1984. 87″ x 110″ (220 x 280 cm). Cottons, some hand-dyed. Machine-pieced. Gunvor is a well-known Swedish textile artist whose pieced hangings attracted the attention of Rolf Bergh, an architect who has designed many churches in Sweden. He visited an exhibition of her work in Stockholm in 1975 and commissioned her to make a series of hangings for a house of refuge that he was building in an old village north of Stockholm. Some years later he approached her again. This time he wanted an altar hanging for a small burial church (*Tacksägelsekyrkan*, a church of thanksgiving), near Lake Vättern in southern Sweden. Gunvor explains that she wanted to create a meditative piece to give a feeling of both peace and joy. "There is a cross in the center surrounded by radiating oval spheres of light. I have always liked geometric designs, because I love the strength you can achieve by working with color within a structured form." Later on, plans were changed and the church became a Congregational church, but Gunvor's design was still appropriate, and she was delighted when Rolf Bergh took some of the colors from her hanging for other furnishings in the interior. Gunvor does not quilt her work and many of her pieces were bought by the Foreign Ministry and now hang in Swedish embassies all over the world. (Photograph courtesy Rolf Dahlström)

England

33. *The Resurrection Cope and Miter*
designed and made by Beryl Dean,
London, England. 1988. Velvet, felt,
suede, silk, organza, gold lamé, imitation gold leather, other gold and black
fabrics. Hand-pieced. British ecclesiastical design has been transformed
through the efforts of one particular
artist, Beryl Dean, the maker of this
magnificent patchwork cope. Beryl
learned ecclesiastical embroidery as
part of her training, but did not pursue it
until 1955 when she realized that the
advances in secular embroidery design
were not being reflected in church
work. Since then she has dedicated
herself to promoting a contemporary
approach to liturgical design and has
written eight books on the subject. She
has taught at many colleges of art in
England, and her influence can be
detected in much of the exciting
modern work to be found in British
churches today. Beryl's favorite maxim
is "find inspiration through your fabric," and when she designed this
beautiful cope, she was led by the tones
and textures of the black and gold
fabrics that she had collected over the
years. She explains that the coloring
symbolizes "the progress of life which
moves from the dense black at the
bottom of the cope, representing
original sin, through the neutral gray of
living towards the light of everlasting
life illustrated by the gold and white of
the miter." She made the cope for the
Reverend Canon Peter Delaney of All
Hallows by the Tower, a church near
the Tower of London. (Photograph
courtesy the artist and Noel Manchee,
London)

34. *Altar Frontal* designed and made by Beryl Dean, assisted by Elizabeth Elvin and Ethel Stevens, for the Interdenominational Chapel at Westminster Hospital, London. 1969. 39″ x 108″ (99 x 274 cm). Silk, metallic tissues, net, velvet, dupion. Hand-pieced. Although Beryl has undertaken many important commissions in Britain and the United States, including a set of copes for the enthronement of a former Archbishop of Canterbury and a set of five superb embroidered panels for St. George's Chapel in Windsor Castle, she says that this handsome patchwork frontal remains one of her favorite pieces. "The reredos is a large painting by Veronese and to complement it I aimed for the sort of colors that are seen on Limoges enamels. I wanted to achieve a kind of restrained richness." Although she was not the first person to use patchwork for church furnishings (see fig. 10), she nevertheless popularized it. Traditional English patchwork is worked over paper templates, and the patches are then whipstitched together. When the work is completed, the papers are removed. Beryl devised a variation of this method that is now common practice today in British ecclesiastical work. She makes her templates from interfacing, and these are left in to provide stability. When different weights of fabric are used, such as the velvets and sheers in this piece, she compensates by varying the thickness of the interfacing. For more information see WAYS AND MEANS, section 5a. (Photograph courtesy the artist)

35. *Faith in the City* designed by Jane Lemon, Salisbury, England, and made by the Sarum Group for Salisbury Cathedral. 1986. 39″ x 156″ (99 x 396 cm). Assorted silks and brocades. Hand-appliqué over stiff interfacing and embroidery. In the introduction to this section we saw in figure 19 an illustration of one of England's finest Gothic cathedrals, Salisbury Cathedral in Wiltshire. This superb contemporary frontal was made for a side altar in the cathedral that stands below a window dedicated to the Prisoners of Conscience, which the designer, Jane Lemon, explains forms the linking theme. "The dawn light, falling on the highrise buildings of a modern city anywhere in the world, depicts the Grace of God coming to those who live there, the prisoners of the city." She feels it the duty of the church and the responsibility of every Christian to bring hope to the inner cities of the world. Jane is one of Britain's foremost ecclesiastical designers and embroiderers, and she founded the Sarum Group, a team of semiprofessional embroiderers who take their name from the prehistoric fortress of Old Sarum near Salisbury. Jane began her career in the wardrobe department of the Sadler's Wells theater and then worked as a costume designer for BBC television, where she says she learned a valuable lesson. "In those days I was designing for black and white television so I had to translate color into tonal values, the lights and darks had to be clearly defined." This lesson is evident in the remarkable three-dimensional effect she has managed to create on this magnificent piece. (Photograph by PhotoShades, Salisbury, reproduced by kind permission of the Dean and Chapter of Salisbury Cathedral)

36. *The Lenten Frontal* designed by Jane Lemon and made by the Sarum Group for Salisbury Cathedral, England. 1983. 39″ x 138″ (99 x 350 cm). Natural linens, scrims, and sheer fabrics. Hand appliqué over stiff interfacing with pulled and drawn threadwork in assorted threads and ribbons. This impressive Lenten frontal, symbolizing the earth, is the third in a series representing the elements designed by Jane for the High Altar in Salisbury Cathedral. (The other two frontals represent air and water.) The earth theme is evident in the coloring of this frontal and in the two converging processions of rock-like people who vividly convey the suffering associated with the passion of Our Lord. The theme also links up with the Prisoners of Conscience window (see fig. 35), which can be seen in conjunction with the High Altar. Jane stretches her frontals over a wooden frame to keep them taut, and if they are to be used with a laudian cloth (a throwover cloth that covers the entire altar) such as you see here, she attaches the edges of the laudian cloth to the sides of the frame with Velcro. She works in both patchwork and appliqué, but nearly always uses a stiff interfacing (the sort used to make curtain pelmets) to back her pattern pieces. She says that all the strands of her life—her previous experience in costume design and in teaching embroidery—have finally come together in the ecclesiastical work that she now does. She has completed commissions for many churches in addition to Salisbury Cathedral, including a number in the United States. (Photograph by PhotoShades, Salisbury, reproduced by kind permission of the Dean and Chapter of Salisbury Cathedral).

41

37. *Altar Frontal and Dossal* designed by Sylvia Green and worked by Joan Carr, Florence Hind, Janet Lewthwaite, and Pamela Newton for All Saints Church, Newland, Gloucestershire, England. 1983. Frontal, 42″ x 82″ (107 x 208 cm). Silk, silk organza, lurex fabrics, dupion. Hand-piecing and appliqué over interfacing. All Saints Church is a magnificent Gothic building, almost like a cathedral, set in the middle of a small country village on the Welsh border. It is known as The Cathedral in the Forest, and it was built in A.D. 1200 to serve as a "mission" church to the mining communities in the Forest of Dean. Originally, each of the three chapels served a particular function with a staff of priests, quite separate from the main church and the High Altar. The priests of the Lady Chapel, for which this striking patchwork frontal was made, had the unenviable task of taking the Scriptures to the iron (and later coal) miners deep in the forest—dangerous work in those days! In 1982, the chapel was completely refurbished and the vicar, the Reverend David Addison and his wife, Joy, decided to commission artists and craftsmen to provide furnishings that reflected the twentieth century. Beryl Dean (see figs. 33 and 34) was the key artist, and it was she who visualized creating a pieced frontal for the chapel although she did not undertake the work herself. The task of designing it fell to Sylvia Green, a professionally trained artist and noted ecclesiastical embroiderer, who decided to use multiple shades of blue to complement the Portugese tiles on the floor. Sylvia also embroidered kneelers for the chapel and, with Beryl and Hazel Sims, designed and embroidered four splendid pennants to hang from the chapel ceiling. (Photograph courtesy Paul Smith, Coleford)

38a, 38b. *Festal Chasuble* made by Grace Fincham for Father John Hamblin of Christ Church, Tottenham, London. 1988. Wild silks with glazed cotton lining. Hand-pieced. Grace has made a number of patchwork cushions and coverlets over the years to raise funds for her church and was therefore very pleased when the vicar, Father John Hamblin, asked her to make him a chasuble for his fiftieth birthday on February 2, 1988. (You can see him wearing it in figure 38b.) This is also the date of Candlemas, the festival that celebrates the presentation of Our Lord in the temple and for which white, or festal, vestments are worn. Grace felt that a sunburst in gold and silver would be appropriate and chose two important Christian symbols for her design— the cross superimposed on the Star of Bethlehem, with rays of light radiating out to form the shape of the vestment. She used the traditional English method of piecing over paper templates but did not remove the papers until she had lined the robe because the silk frayed so badly. "I have always been interested in geometric designs since primary school and can become quite obsessional, working into the small hours," Grace says, "and I feel that a striking pattern can be achieved in patchwork by somebody who is not very skilled in embroidery." She confesses that she took up patchwork after she retired from teaching to help cut down her smoking! (Photographs courtesy Noel Manchee, London, and the Reverend John Seeley)

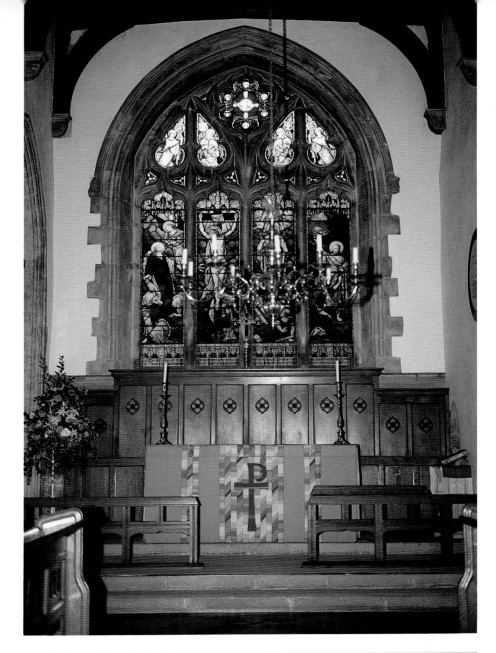

39a, 39b. *Altar Frontal* designed by Jennie Parry for the Church of St. Peter and St. Paul, Great Bowden, Leicestershire. 1988. 38″ x 83″ (95 x 210 cm). Green and red silks. Machine-pieced over interfacing. Jennie's commission from the vicar was to find a way of bringing color to the church on a limited budget, a familiar cry to liturgical designers all over the world! She is a professional embroiderer, but she chose piecework in this instance because it enabled her to achieve a dramatic effect with minimum cost. She worked her design in six shades of red silk and eight shades of green silk, and by cutting her patches both on the straight and on the diagonal so that they reflected the light differently, she was able to create the effect of many more subtle tones. She explains that she wanted the Chi Rho monogram to "float" on the background, so she deliberately kept the coloring of the pieced panel lighter than the monogram as dark colors will always advance on a light background. Although she mounted the main frontal on a stretcher, she did not do so with the super-frontal and admits that she had difficulty in aligning up the patches so that the panels were continuous. "I enjoy working on commissions for the church," Jennie says. "It is an offering of one's skills and the work is useful." Many of her pieces have been hung in both secular and ecclesiastical exhibitions and have also appeared in several books. The frontal was given in memory of W.T. Cotton (1909–1986). (Photographs courtesy the artist)

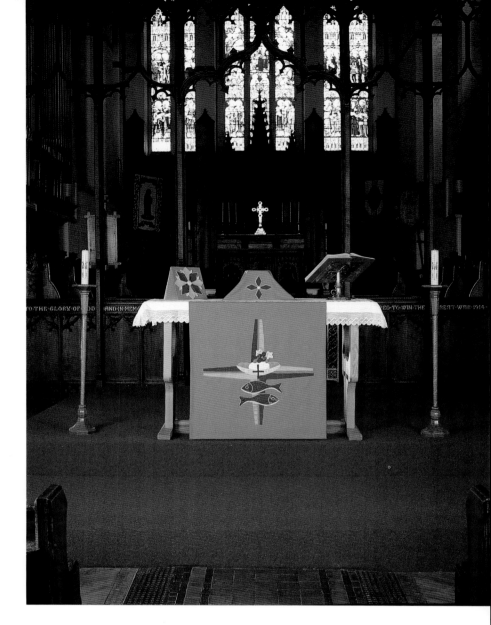

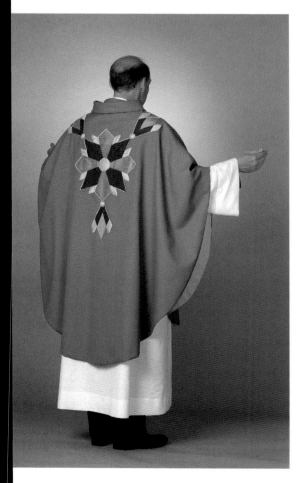

40a, 40b. *Altar Set and Chasuble* designed by Gill Bryan and Barbara Holmes and made by the Sewing Guild for the church of St. Mary Magdalene, Wandsworth Common, London. 1991. 75″ x 36″ (190.8 x 91 cm). Wool and synthetic blend, Thai silks. Hand-piecing and appliqué over interfacing, embroidery. Apart from the structural work, the refurbishment of our Victorian church of St. Mary Magdalene has been a real community project. The new nave altar was made by a member of the congregation, Professor Bryan Brooke (a retired surgeon), from old pews that were removed to make way for the dais. When it came to making a frontal for it, the vicar, the Reverend Ian Kitteringham, wanted a narrow one that would show the lyre-shaped legs, and he also specified that the design must be modern and colorful. Gill Bryan's design of a basket of bread and grapes and fish is superimposed on a divided cross and picks up the coloring of the dais carpet and the stained-glass window behind. The same fabrics were used for the chasuble that is worn by the vicar in figure 40b. Barbara Holmes's design was pieced in sections and then applied. To complete the set, Dora Littlechild and her daughter Barbara made 220 inches (550 cm) of bobbin lace to edge the "fair linen" altar cloth. The other members of the Sewing Guild who were involved are Pauline Charlton, Barbara Hill, Jean Hills, Jill Jeffery, Violet Plume, Joan Watts, and the author. The set was given in memory of Freda Rowe and Arthur Tomlinson. (Photographs courtesy Noel Manchee, London)

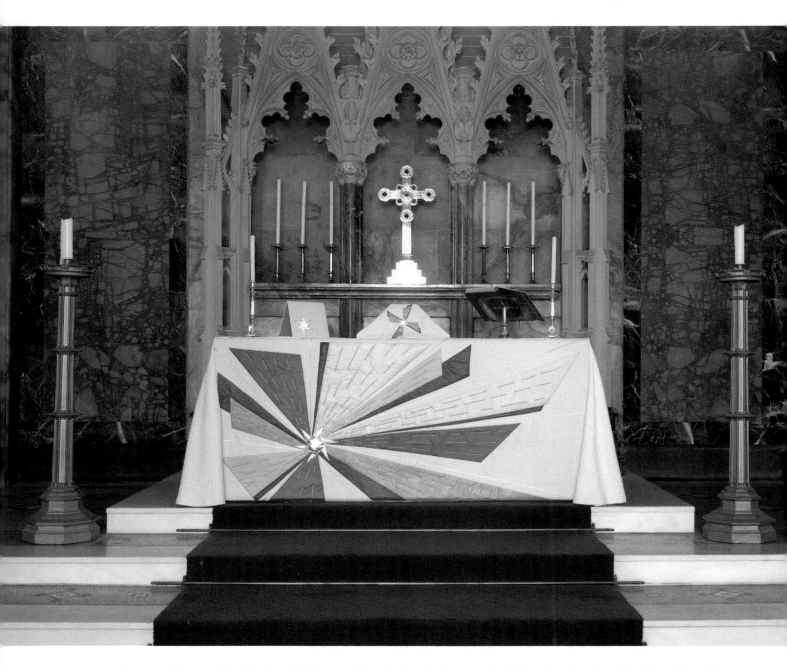

41. *Festal Frontal* designed by Barbara Holmes and made by the Sewing Guild for the church of St. Mary Magdalene, Wandsworth Common, London. 1993. 37″ x 84″ (94 x 213.8 cm). Cotton-linen mix, chintz, gold cording, and braid. Hand-appliqué and embroidery. Although the nave altar at St. Mary Magdalene is used for most of the year, during the festive seasons of Easter and Christmas, and for Trinity Sunday the High Altar becomes the focus of worship. When she designed this dramatic frontal, Barbara says that she wanted to create a feeling of energy, of powerful forces emanating from a single source. "I wanted it to be joyful too, a celebration of the Resurrection and of the expansion of Christianity throughout the world." We used chintzes in various colors backed with curtain interlining for the "rays," which were couched by members of the sewing group with gold braid (we used a bodkin to insert the braid through the layers). Then the rays were applied to a fabric base, which we stiffened and backed, and suspended over a throwover laudian cloth that creates soft folds at the sides. (Directions for making a suspended frontal and a laudian cloth can be found in WAYS AND MEANS, section 9). In keeping with her theme of spiritual dynamism, Barbara chose to make a cog the focal point on the frontal instead of the more traditional cross. "I wasn't sure how this would be received by the congregation," she explains, "but our vicar, Ian Kitteringham, liked the idea, and I think most people have accepted it with good grace!" Seen from the body of the church, the cog (made from gold kid) appears numinous in the candlelight. (Photograph courtesy Noel Manchee, London)

42a, 42b. *Baptistry Banners* designed by Gill Bryan and made by the Sewing Guild for the church of St. Mary Magdalene, Wandsworth Common, London. 1990. 57″ x 32″ (145 x 81.4 cm). Cotton furnishing fabric, damask, chintz, sequins. Hand-piecing, appliqué, and embroidery. As mentioned in figure 40, the refurbishment of our church, a gaunt Victorian building, has been very much a "do-it-yourself" affair. The Sewing Guild was formed originally to do repair work, notably to mend the old vestments and the tattered banners in the chancel. Then our vicar, Ian Kitteringham, asked us to make something "colorful" for the west end of the church, which was a challenging expanse of blank white wall with the disadvantage of a large leaking window above it! Inspiration can come from many sources, and for Gill Bryan, who is the wife of the sacristan, it was an illustration of a sixteenth-century Japanese kimono that inspired the stunning design of naturalistic lilies in figure 42a. Lilies are a symbol of purity and are associated with the Virgin Mary. As these banners were to hang on either side of the baptismal font, Gill chose bulrushes, which signify salvation, for the second banner (fig. 42b), and she thus succeeded in representing both the New and the Old Testaments. Every member of the Sewing Guild worked on some part of these banners (we used sequins for the top-knots on the bulrushes), and we tried to alleviate the problem of the damp by hanging them on wooden brackets that stood out from the wall. The banners, however, received several soakings before the window was repaired, but the fabrics stood up well. The banners were given in memory of Ronald Holmes. (Photographs courtesy Noel Manchee, London)

43a, 43b, 43c, 43d. *Pillar Pennants* designed by Gill Bryan, Carolyn Clough, and John Plume, and made by the Sewing Guild for the church of St. Mary Magdalene, Wandsworth Common, London. 1992. 52″ x 18″ (132.3 x 46.8 cm). Deckchair canvas, cottons, silks, chintz. Hand-appliqué and embroidery. In our efforts to liven up the interior of St. Mary Magdalene, we have hung pennants on four of the six pillars in the nave (two more are in the pipeline). The plan is to make several different sets that can be rotated according to the church seasons. We used deckchair canvas for these pennants and found it to be very successful. The narrow width was ideal, it hangs well, and seems not to be affected by humidity, unlike some cotton furnishing fabrics. The attractive designs, drawn by professional and amateur artists in the congregation, continue the botanical theme set by the lily and bulrush banners in figures 42a and 42b, which is appropriate because the church is situated in a particularly "leafy" part of London. The tasseled cords are curtain tie-backs bought from a decorator shop, and we made the rods from lengths of doweling with small wooden knobs screwed to each end, an idea that we copied from Barbara Featherstone, whose work is illustrated in figure 45. (Photographs courtesy Noel Manchee, London)

 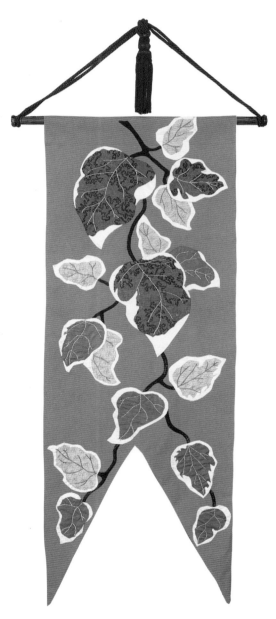

43a. *Pomegranates* (designed by Carolyn Clough) are a sign of the Resurrection and, because of the unity of so many seeds in one fruit, the pomegranate also symbolizes the church.

43b. *Ivy* (designed by John Plume) represents eternal life and also fidelity because of the way it clings to a support. John painted the yellow part of the leaves with fabric paint.

43c. *Wheat* (designed by Gill Bryan) symbolizes bountifulness and also the bread of the Eucharist.

43d. *Grapes* (designed by John Plume) denotes the Eucharistic wine. We used a variety of fabrics for the grapes and stuffed each one with batting to create a three-dimensional effect.

44a. *Pentecost Banner* designed by Barbara Littlechild and made by the Sewing Guild for the church of St. Mary Magdalene, Wandsworth Common, London. 1991. 52″ x 28″ (132 x 71 cm). Viscose and cottons, gold cord. Hand-appliqué and embroidery. Our aim is to have a banner for each of the church seasons that will hang just inside the porch and welcome the congregation as they come in. We have only achieved two so far, this inspirational Pentecost banner and one for Christmas (see fig. 44b). Barbara Littlechild chose the classic symbols of a dove and flames to represent the Holy Spirit, and in order to convey the idea of the Holy Spirit pouring out on the heads of people of all nations we machine-stitched lines of gold cord to the background. The lettering was stuck on with double-sided fusible interfacing, and we couched wool around each one and also around the dove. (Photograph courtesy Noel Manchee, London)

44b. *Christmas Banner* designed by Gill Bryan from a drawing by Bev Saunders. 1991. 53″ x 36″ (135 x 91 cm). American calicoes, silk, silver tissue, imitation gold and silver leather, fur fabric, cords, braid, and wool. Hand-appliqué, quilting, and trapunto. All the classic quilting techniques were used in this Christmas banner, which has been much admired by the congregation. Gill adapted her design from a charity Christmas card that artist Bev Saunders drew for Cancer Research in 1990. Christmas cards provide a wonderful source of ideas, but if you plan to copy a design you should try and obtain the permission of the artist. Bev was so pleased to hear that her illustration would live on in the form of a church banner! Each member of the Sewing Guild was responsible for one panel and for finding the right kind of wool for the beards and hair, and suitable fabrics for the accessories. (Photograph courtesy Noel Manchee, London)

45. *Christ in You, the Hope of Glory* designed by Barbara Featherstone and made by twenty-six members of the congregation for Queens Road Baptist Church, Wimbledon, England. 1988. 8′ x 12′ (3.65 m x 2.43 m). Gold lurex, silks, polyester, viscose, glazed cotton, satin, embossed fabrics. Machine-piecing. When Queen's Road Baptist Church vacated the old Victorian building in Wimbledon and built a new church further down the road, Barbara Featherstone was asked to design a hanging for it that would involve as many of the congregation as possible. She prayed for guidance and received the words "Christ in us," which she then looked up in a concordance. She found the text from Colossians 1:27 "Christ in you, the hope of glory" and she based her design on this. She says, "I was excited by the fact that Paul was speaking about how he gave himself to the church and as this was to be a group project, I felt the two things were related." She decided on patchwork because it was easy to build up blocks of color in the shape of crosses and to use color symbolically. She gave each of the twenty-six members of her team (including one man) a strip of squares to machine at home but did the assembling herself. She says it was an enormous task and "took months to do. I couldn't get to the closets in our bedroom without difficulty, neither could my poor husband!" But her efforts were rewarded, the hanging is a triumph. The striking design reads from the bottom left to the top right as follows: Black—sin, Brown—repentance, Red—sacrifice of the Cross, Violet—suffering, Green—new life in Jesus, Blue—heavenly truth, Yellow—heaven, White—purity, Gold—glory, Gray—humility. (Photograph courtesy Alan Wendelken, London)

46a, 46b. *Falls for Each Side of the Altar* designed and made by Aileen Murray, Seaford, Sussex, England, for the Meeting House Chapel at Sussex University. 1982. 48″ x 48″ (122 x 122 cm). Furnishing fabrics, dupions, and velvets on a linen union interlining. Machine-pieced. We have already seen how a Danish liturgical artist, Tove Basse, used the Log Cabin pattern for a chasuble in figures 30a and 30b, and here is another fascinating interpretation by a professional textile artist in England. Aileen Murray was commissioned to design two hangings for the modern meeting house in Sussex University. She was specifically asked to relate her work to the windows that contain red and yellow glass on one side, and green and yellow on the other. The church is ecumenical so she chose an appropriate text from the order for Holy Communion, "Though we are many, we are one body, because we all share in one bread." Relating the design to the building in style, color, and ideas expressed is always Aileen's first consideration. "I also felt that a design which used many small pieces expressed the idea of the Meeting House. The many small parts together are part of one design just as many people are part of one church." She began by machining small rectangles of different colored fabrics to the background, using a close zigzag stitch, and then applied the Log Cabin crosses, having first worked them on muslin. Aileen says she has become increasingly involved with church commissions at a time of growth and development in her own faith. (Photographs courtesy the artist)

47. *Come Holy Spirit* designed by Doreen Walker and made by Julie James and Catherine Ingram-Smith with help from other members of the congregation for St. Laurence's Church, Upton, Slough, England. 1989. 72″ x 48″ (183 x 122 cm). Cottons, dupion, polyester, corduroy, and felt. Hand and machine-appliqué. St. Laurence's church has always been held in great affection by its congregation and even though it is now situated on a traffic circle on the outskirts of an industrial city, it has been completely refurbished inside and is still the center of a worshiping community. When Doreen Walker designed this superb banner to hang in the sanctuary, she wanted to convey this affection, and so she shows the church as it is today, surrounded by highrise buildings, but blessed by the Holy Spirit in the form of a descending dove. (You can see the symbol for a traffic circle beside a yew tree that is believed to be 800 years old.) The original church was Saxon, although no trace of it remains today, and the present stone building dates from the early 1100s. In the late eighteenth century, the church fell into disrepair and was later restored with funds provided by the congregation, but it was during its period of dilapidation that it caught the eye of the poet Thomas Gray (1716–1771), who almost certainly wrote his famous "Elegy in a Country Churchyard" with St. Laurence's in mind. The "ivy-mantled tow'r" was indeed a landmark, and the "curfew bell that tolls the knell of parting day," could in those quieter days be heard across the fields at Eton College. The making of the banner was a real community project, and tremendous efforts were made by all those involved to find just the right fabric for each architectural feature. (Photograph courtesy Noel Manchee, London)

 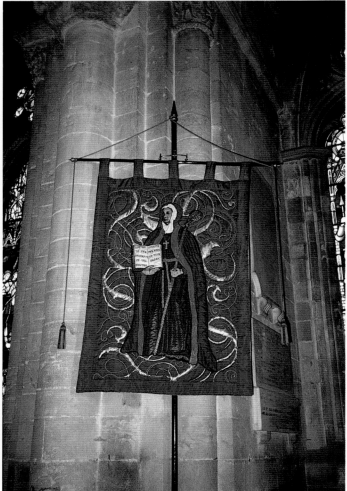

48a, 48b. *Patronal Banners* designed by Jon Crane and made by June Thorpe, Joyce Downer, Elizabeth Kelley, Margaret Spreadbury, Pheobe Bartleet, and Jo Hayes for Romsey Abbey, Hampshire, England. 1989. 59″ x 35½″ (150 x 90 cm). Silks, rayons, viscose, cottons, polyester. Machine-appliqué. The Abbey of St. Mary and St. Ethelfleda in Romsey is a fine Norman church that was constructed in the early 1100s on the site of a Benedictine nunnery, and has been very little altered since that time. The town in those days could afford such an important church because of the prosperity brought to the area by the wool trade. The banners, shown in their normal position against the massive pillars of the abbey, are of the two patron saints, the Virgin Mary seen with her mother, St. Anne (fig. 48a), and St. Ethelfleda (fig. 48b), who was the first abbess of the original nunnery. They are part of a set that was made by a group working under the leadership of June Thorpe, a well-known British quilter who owns a quilt shop in the town. "The sharing of skills is very important to me," June says, "and to be able to use my talents to help beautify a magnificent old church like the abbey is very satisfying." (Photographs courtesy June Thorpe)

49. *Sunset Cross* by Josephine Ratcliff, Preston, Lancashire, England, for the Church of St. John, Preston. 1991. 54″ x 36″ (137 x 91 cm). Glazed chintz, cotton, gold braid. Strip-piecing, hand-appliqué, and embroidery. "I am not sure which came first, the evocative quotation from *Poems for the Fallen* by Laurence Binyon (1869–1943), which is always read before the Last Post [Taps], 'At the going down of the sun and in the morning, we will remember them,' or the desire to create a Celtic cross set against a sunset landscape," says the maker of this beautiful banner that now hangs in the chapel of the Queen's Loyal Lancashire Regiment in Preston Parish Church. "For me, the piece commemorates the ever-growing company of my friends who 'go before me' and whom I remember with joy and gratitude for their lives, their friendship, and their example—as well as those who gave their life for their country." One of those whom Josephine wanted to commemorate especially was her first patchwork teacher, Sue Belton, who died of cancer aged fifty-three in January 1991. ("She taught me the basic building blocks of my craft.") The sunset background is strip-pieced, and the lovely Celtic knot-work was done by hand with gold braid. Josephine's "signature" is the exquisite hand-embroidered lettering that she usually incorporates in all her work. Her husband, Christopher, does the original calligraphy for her. The roses along the bottom are the emblem of the regiment, and these are also hand-embroidered. (Photograph courtesy Christopher Ratcliff, Preston)

50. *Door Curtain* designed and made by Mary Fogg with thirteen helpers from the congregation for St. Katherine's Church, Merstham, Surrey, England. 1989. 133″ x 85″ (338 x 216 cm). Mixed woolen cloths, cotton backing, blanket interlining. Machined-pieced and quilted. What better way to end the English section of our "pilgrimage" than with this marvelous textured curtain made to keep out the draft in a 600-year-old church! Mary Fogg is a well-known professional quilt artist, who is noted for her strip-pieced work that she makes mostly from recycled fabrics. The curtain over the west door of her church was worn out, and Mary undertook to make a replacement assisted by other members of the parish. She says that the design, materials, and colors seemed to select themselves. "I had to take into account that the curtain would be the dominant feature for communicants returning to their seats from the altar, and since the font stands immediately in front of it, the curtain also had to provide a suitable background for baptisms. The old roughened stone and the need for warmth suggested textured wool, and there is a stained-glass window above the door that is predominantly blue, green, and red. I thought about using a representational design of a descending dove, but felt it was better to follow the simple Gothic lines of the church. I collected all the good-quality tweed scraps I could find—charity shops were a good source—but the bright window colors, particularly the blues, could only be captured with the dye-pot. Fortunately, I found a mill that was willing to sell me some undyed cloth that I could color with acid dyes." The group pinned the strips to the backing and batting, and then Mary machined them down, stitching through all three layers. "It was hard going, but it was exciting when the curtain was finally hung in place—I felt it was a contemporary contribution to the beauty of an ancient place of worship." (Photograph courtesy Noel Manchee, London)

France

51a, 51b. *Restored Banner* by Mariel Clarmont, Paris, France, for the Church of St. Rémy, Louâtre. 1985. 39" x 27½" (100 x 70 cm). Dralon, eighteenth-century embroidery, silk fringe. Hand-quilted. The pilgrimage to France produced two fascinating examples of the way in which French quiltmakers are helping to preserve their national heritage. In this photograph you can see how Mariel Clarmont, a Parisian artist, has salvaged an eighteenth-century embroidery from a banner that was falling to bits and given it new life by framing it with rich contour quilting. The original banner hung in a church at Louâtre, which is a small country village of some two hundred inhabitants north of Paris that lies in the ancient duchy of Valois. Parts of the church date back to the eleventh century and when it was apparent that the French government department Monuments Historiques refused to repair the tattered banners, the Mayor of Louâtre, M. Jean Maurice, asked Mariel to find a way of saving them. A second banner is in course of restoration. The mayor lent the charming old postcard of the church that you can see in figure 51b. The photograph of the church was taken about 1910, and soon thereafter the church was badly damaged by bombing in World War I. (Photograph of banner courtesy Studio 80, Paris)

52. *Restored Altar Panel* by Marta Jeannine, Montfermeil, France, for the Church of St. Pierre, St. Paul, Montfermeil. 1989. 47″ x 39″ (120 x 100 cm). Antique embroidery and gold brocade, jeweled stones, colored lamé. Hand-pieced and embroidered. Like her compatriot Mariel Clarmont, Marta Jeannine wanted to preserve the beautiful embroideries from some old, fragile chasubles belonging to her local church that were no longer wearable. Because she is a keen patchworker, she decided to set the embroidered cross against an exquisitely colored, pieced panel worked in shimmering lamé in a variation of the Drunkard's Path pattern. She used iron-on interfacing to support the patches, for the lamé was also fragile, and then she stitched green and gold cords around each quarter circle. "I did it to praise God," she says, "and although it was difficult work—I had to redo the encrustation of jewels on the cross and replace the missing stones—it was a marvelous feeling to have been able to repair these holy things." The panel is part of a set that includes a plain white altar cloth on which Marta applied another gold cross, and it is used in the oratory where Mass is celebrated every day. Marta was apprenticed at the age of thirteen to a Parisian *couture* house, and she worked subsequently for both the House of Dior and Jean-Louis Scherrer. In consequence, she grew to love textiles, and so when she retired in 1985, she decided to devote her time to patchwork. Another of her hangings appears in figure 53. (Photograph courtesy Philippe Darmengeat)

53. *Nativité* by Marta Jeannine, Montfermeil, France, after a painting by Henri de Montrond. 1987. 91″ x 59″ (230 x 150 cm). Cottons. Hand-appliqué and quilting. In addition to preserving precious antique vestments (see fig. 33), Marta Jeannine also makes modern religious hangings, and we end our European pilgrimage with her wonderful *Nativité*. She took her inspiration from a painting by Henri de Montrond, a designer of prayer books, who is at present working on a decorative project for Tours Cathedral. It was the symbolism of the piece, the worship of the infant Jesus by people of all races, that Marta found enthralling, and she was delighted when M. de Montrond not only gave her permission to use his design but also advised her on the coloring. She made a full-scale drawing first and gave each pattern piece a number and also noted the coloring. Then she transferred the design to tissue paper and basted this to the black cotton background. As she applied each piece of fabric, she pulled away the tissue paper from behind. She sewed the finished piece to white cotton and then quilted it. The banner hung in her local Church of St. Pierre, St. Paul at Montfermeil for four years, but then the *curé* (the priest) decided that it should circulate to each of the churches in the parish at Christmas time. Marta loves this type of work and says that her training in *haut-couture* has given her the audacity to do it! (Photograph courtesy Vincent Marta)

A Pilgrim's Guide to North America: United States and Canada

Probably no continent in the world has produced so much diversity of religious thought and expression as North America. The sturdy individualism that characterized the early settlers blended with the streams of immigrants from different cultures to produce an amazing proliferation of ideas and practices in religion. This rich kaleidoscope gives inspiration to the many quilters who devote their skills to the embellishment of their churches or to the expression of spiritual feelings.

The diversity began with the earliest settlements from Europe. The Spanish brought Roman Catholicism to Mexico and Florida in the early 1500s. Captain John Smith planted the Church of England in Virginia. Maryland was a refuge for English Catholics. Swedish Lutherans and Dutch Protestants settled New Sweden and New Netherlands. The English Puritans came to New England in the early 1600s. The French brought Roman Catholicism to Newfoundland, Montreal, and Nova Scotia, which was known in those days as Arcadia. Later, the Arcadians spread down the Mississippi to Louisiana, where they became known as "Cajuns." By 1650, the religious diversity was already becoming evident.

The first church to be established in the English colonies was the Church of England in Virginia. The expedition sent out by the Virginia Council of London landed on the southern shore of Chesapeake Bay on April 26, 1607, and set up a cross to mark the place of landing. It was here that they subsequently built a fort and, according to the diary of Captain John Smith, the first church was a makeshift affair. "...We did hang an awneing (which is an old saile) to three of four trees, to shadow us from the sunne; our walls were rales of wood; our seats unhewed trees till we cut plankes, our pulpit a bar of wood.... In foule weather we shifted into an old rotten tent.... This was our church till we built a homely thing like a barne. Yet we had daily Common Prayer, morning and evening; every Sunday two sermons and every three months the Holy Communion, till our minister died..."[17]

The second English settlement was by the Puritans in 1620 at Plymouth, Massachusetts, and soon after landing the Puritans erected a meeting house. This was constructed on a hill near the harbor and was a large square building on which the Pilgrim Fathers wisely mounted six cannon as a defense against the native Indians. In those early and dangerous days, guns were also much in evidence during the church services (fig. 54).

The Pilgrims constituted only a small proportion of the New England Puritans, and were the only body that from the first advocated separation from the Church of England. Later immigrants desired to stay within the church "but to do away with its forms and ceremonies, to reduce the power of the bishops and to expel from the church people of 'ungodly' life."[18]

This last aspiration led to outright discrimination. According to Aymar Embury II, in his book *Early American Churches*, in order to become a burgess with the right to vote, "one had to belong to one of the churches established by law in New England, but the church elected new members (like a club), rejecting those unfit for Christian fellowship (and it was astonishing how little made a man unfit). But the fact that a man was not permitted to join a church...did not mean that he was free from taxation or that he did not have to go to church. Oh, no indeed. He had to attend church just as faithfully as any church member and behave with the same decorum, or else be whipped and fined."[19]

The American Revolution in 1776 brought change and innovation. From being just branches of European institutions, the various churches in the United States were remolded as indigenous churches in an independent state. In some cases this was a painful process. The Anglican church almost destroyed itself over the problem of Episcopal succession in forming new Episcopal churches.

The career of Samuel Seabury is an illustration. After the Revolution, the English bishops would have nothing to do with the breakaway American Episcopal Church in Connecticut that wanted him as its bishop, so he was consecrated by Scottish bishops in Aberdeen in 1784. You can see from his portrait in figure 55 the balanced intelligence that informed the founders of the United States in the late 1700s.

Protestant clergy were vested very simply at this period: cassocks, black Geneva-type gowns and bands and plain white surplices were worn for the most part. Communion tables, rather than altars, were used and these were covered with a simple "fair linen" cloth.

In figure 55 Bishop Seabury is seen dressed typically as a bishop of the day in chimere and rochet with neck and wristbands. (A chimere is a bishop's outer robe, and the name possibly comes from the Spanish *zamarra*, meaning "a sheepskin cloak"; a rochet is a billowy surplice.) These vestments were almost certainly purchased in England.

He also owned and used a miter (fig. 56), although no other bishop in the Anglican church in either Britain or America had done so since the Reformation, and this miter forms a link with Thomas John Claggett, bishop of the separate Episcopal Church of Maryland. Seabury had consecrated Claggett, but the southerners would not accept a Scottish line of succession, so Claggett had to be consecrated again in New York under the English line, and thus united the two successions. Claggett owned a replica of Seabury's miter, made for him by Seabury's daughter Maria, perhaps to symbolize the healing of the schism.

Both miters are still in existence and are another example of the way the church has created vestments from secular clothing. They were converted from silk stove-pipe hats with the brims removed and the crowns partly cut out!

Such vestments as were worn in the United States during the early days were imported from England. Miters began to be used again in the American Episcopal

54. Worship during the early days of settlement was a dangerous affair. Soon after they landed at Plymouth in 1620, the Puritans built a meeting house on a hill near the harbor. On the roof they mounted six cannon, and during church services, guns were very much in evidence, as you can see from this colored engraving entitled *Public Worship at Plymouth*. A house of worship was required to have a pulpit toward the middle of one wall, and although the position of the altar in the early meeting house is not documented, records show that later on it came to be placed in front of the pulpit. Protestant denominations in America tended to use a communion table adorned with a simple white cloth rather than an altar. (Photograph courtesy Bettmann Archives, New York)

church around 1880 in some of the more Anglo-Catholic dioceses, and today are quite commonplace, indeed almost universally worn. American vestment manufacture seems to have come into being around 1882.

After the Revolution, denominations other than the Anglican church had similar difficulties in remolding themselves. The Methodists at that time were a religious society dependant upon the Church of England, but the Church of England would not ordain priests for service in the rebellious colonies, so John Wesley (1703–1791) took the task upon himself. This led to the creation of the separate Methodist Episcopal Church, although Wesley himself never left the Church of England. Presbyterians, Congregationalists, Calvinists, and Catholics all went through a similar metamorphosis.

In the late eighteenth century a new spirit of revivalism known as "The Second Great Awakening" affected the American churches. The spur was the frontier, receding ever westward, and the need for missionary work among the pioneers. Yale University was the birthplace. Timothy Dwight, president of the university from 1795 to 1817, and his pupil Lyman Beecher inspired the Awakening. Beecher's daughters, Catherine and Harriet, were both to play central roles in the history of the United States.

Traditionally, slaves worshiped in their masters' churches (fig. 57), but in 1787, a freed slave from Philadelphia, Richard Allen, formed a segregated black church that became the African Methodist Episcopal church. Many separate black denominations were to follow in a movement that has vigor to this day. Other new religious denominations made their appearance—the Shakers, Universalists (fig. 58), Unitarians, and Free Will Baptists were all inspired at this time by revivalist sentiment.

As the nineteenth century progressed, there was a widening spectrum of religious expression. A stream of immigrants—German and Scandinavian Lutherans, and the Dutch—affected the American versions of their churches. The influx of Roman Catholics led the Roman Catholic church from being one of the smallest denominations to become the largest single denomination by mid-century. The Church of Jesus Christ of the Latter Day Saints (the Mormons), founded by Joseph Smith, expressed the independence and nonconformity of the American personality. But in all denominations, the church remained the center of the community, the heart of American life just as it had been since the days of the founding fathers (fig. 59).

In religious expression in the early 1800s, the role of women was seen in the light of "the dictum of the Apostle Paul that they should keep silent in the Church."[20] But women began to make a breakthrough in the field of education. Catherine Beecher founded the National Board of Popular Education that sent many teachers into the South and West.

Catherine Beecher's younger sister, Harriet Beecher Stowe, had a different impact. Her novel, *Uncle Tom's Cabin*, published in 1852, aroused popular horror against slavery and this became a factor in the sad sequence leading to the Civil War. Despite Saint Paul, women played a prominent part in the life of the nation.

Meanwhile, in Canada the life of the churches moved at a gentler pace. Robert T. Hardy, in his book *A History of the Churches in the United States and Canada*, comments, "Canadian Christianity on the whole was more conservative and adhered more closely to European traditions than did the Americans."[21]

From the colonial powers, Canada received the Church of England as an "Established" official church, but in 1852, the church was disestablished, thus putting it on a level footing with other churches. The Canadian Anglicans learned early that it was healthier to be self-supporting rather than being subsidized by the state. Presbyterianism from Scotland came to the Maritime Provinces. From France came a strain of Roman Catholicism that rejected the French Revolution and preserved beloved traditions of the past. It has been the binding force of French-speaking Canada ever since.

The twentieth century plunged into World War II in 1939, from which the United States emerged in 1945 as a superpower, champion of the free world against the Communist ideology. Canada found a complementary role as spokesman for the smaller powers. There was a strong revival of religion in the 1950s, of which an enduring phenomenon is the heartfelt evangelism of Dr. Billy Graham. New ideas also abounded in the Roman Catholic Church, culminating in Vatican 11, but the revival lost momentum in the 1960s and 1970s.

In the ebb and flow of religious enthusiasm that marks our century, it seems that the flow may be with us again. Certainly, the involvement of the laity in the churches is encouraging, as this book witnesses. American quilters have reveled in the diversity of their heritage to create a wonderfully variegated body of work, and if the denominational spectrum is smaller in Canada, their quilters have been no less inspired.

ANDREW LIDDELL

55. In this 1785 portrait by Ralph Earle, Bishop Samuel Seabury (1729–1796), one of America's early bishops, is wearing the typical vestments of a bishop of the time—an outer robe known as a chimere over a rochet (a type of billowing surplice). These vestments would have been imported from England, as American vestment manufacture did not begin until the 1880s. (Photograph courtesy the Reverend Dr. Robert G. Carroon, Archivist and Historiographer of the Episcopal Diocese of Connecticut)

56. This miter is a marvelous illustration of the way in which church authorities successfully turned secular garments into vestments. It was made for Bishop Seabury from a silk stovepipe hat by a Mr. Stone, possibly in London. The brim was removed and the crown was cut out to form the distinctive points. As no bishop in England wore a miter at that time, nobody knew how to make them, but Charles Inglis (who eventually became the first Bishop of Nova Scotia) took control. In a letter dated London, September 14, 1786 (now owned by Trinity College, Hartford, Connecticut), Charles Inglis explains how he told Stone "... that he must try his Hand. He and I have consulted together at least a Dozen times: & we also called in a very ingenious Embroiderer to assist us."[22] Bishop Seabury wore his miter for services, something no other bishop was to do in the United States for nearly a hundred years, and a copy was made by Seabury's daughter, Maria, for her father to give to Bishop Thomas John Claggett of Maryland. However, it is not known for certain whether or not Bishop Claggett ever wore his miter, but the fact that these two eighteenth-century American bishops owned the only miters in the Anglican church since the Reformation is a fascinating fragment of history. Both miters are still in existence and are owned by the respective dioceses of Connecticut and Maryland. (Photograph courtesy the Reverend Dr. Robert G. Carroon, Archivist and Historiographer of the Episcopal Diocese of Connecticut)

57. African-American slave quilts are an important part of quilting history in America, particularly the Bible quilts made by Harriet Powers who was born into slavery in 1837. Here is another type of slave quilt that was made for religious celebration. Traditionally, slaves worshiped in their masters' churches, and in the last century it was the custom for the Bishop of New Orleans to pay an annual visit to the Mimosa Hall Plantation in Texas in order to perform baptisms, confirmations, and marriages. Each time the bishop came, it was customary to make a quilt in his honor, hence the charming design of chalices in this quilt. Everybody helped, including the children and the slaves. After the bishop departed, it is thought that the quilt was used by the children, or by the slaves themselves. Cotton, 1860. (Photograph courtesy the American Museum in Britain, Bath, England)

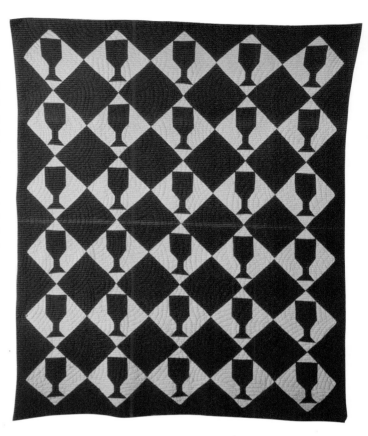

58. Unitarianism is a denomination with a strong intellectual base deriving from eighteenth-century Harvard University. Its emphasis is on the single personality of God (as opposed to the more usual Trinitarian concept), which caused some controversy during the mid 1800s. However, its ability to assimilate modern scientific thought made it adaptable, and it has found an accommodation today with other denominations. The First Church of Deerfield in Massachusetts is a Federated congregation of the United Church of Christ and the Unitarian Universalist Association. At the time of the controversy in the nineteenth century, the parish split and a second church was founded in Deerfield. During World War II, the two congregations met for united services and after the war, the two churches merged again and took the legal name of The First Church of Deerfield. The church is a beautiful example of an indigenous American classical architectural style called Federal. (Photograph by Helga Photo Studio)

59. At the beginning of the nineteenth century, the church was the center of the community, the heart of American life. In this extraordinary appliqué quilt made by Sarah Furman Warner of Greenfield Hill, Connecticut, in 1800, the church with its tall spire stands firmly in the middle of the picture. The citizens of the small New England village parade in front of the church and around the edge of the medallion you can see other details of this idealized rural life: a chicken coop, a windmill, and a horse-drawn buggy. (Henry Ford Museum and Greenfield Village, Dearborn, Michigan)

United States

60a, 60b, 60c. *Reversible Altar Cloths and Pulpit Hangings* by Joy Saville, Princeton, New Jersey, United States. 1986. Our pilgrimage to North America begins in the United States with some intriguing furnishings made for the Nassau Presbyterian Church in Princeton. When Joy Saville, textile artist and Church Elder, was commissioned to make a set of altar cloths and pulpit hangings for the eight seasons of the church year, she chose to do it in a most ingenious manner. She made four altar cloths in a cruciform shape in the four liturgical colors of red, green, purple, and white and worked them so that each one can be reversed to serve another season. The pulpit falls are also reversible. Figure 60a shows the side of the green cloth that is used for the Sundays after Pentecost, while figure 60b reveals its other face, Sundays after Epiphany. Figure 60c is the cloth that is used for Pentecost itself, and this cloth has Palm Sunday on its reverse side. The other two (not illustrated) are the purple Advent/Lent cloth and the white Christmas/Eastertide. Before she began her task, Joy asked herself, "How do I make the sacred visible?" She felt that the communion table itself is a symbol so she did not want to overload a symbolic object with more symbols. "Color itself is a symbol; it expresses concepts and feelings. Patterns can be quiet or active. Each season has its own spirit—this is what I tried to express through color." She used piecework for three of the cloths, but felt that the passion of Palm Sunday and Pentecost called for organic, flowing lines that were better executed in appliqué. Joy knew that the damp weather in Princeton was likely to have an effect on the behavior of the cloths, so she did not quilt them, preferring to let them hang freely and, because the main focus of worship in the Presbyterian church is a communion table (rather than an altar), she left the corners of the white undercloth open, thus allowing the table to be seen. This silk-linen undercloth also serves as a backdrop for the colored cloths and visually unifies the table with the white pulpit. (Photographs courtesy William Taylor, Princeton)

60b. *Sundays after Epiphany.* Altar cloth: 80″ x 113″ (203 x 287 cm). Pulpit hanging: 30″ x 22″ (76 x 56 cm). Silk, cotton, corduroy. Seminole patchwork. This is the other side of the cloth in figure 60a.

60c. *Palm Sunday/Pentecost cloth.* (Same dimensions as for fig. 60b). This is the Pentecost side of this vivid appliqué cloth. On the Palm Sunday side, the flames are grouped to create the effect of palm branches.

61a, 61b, 61c. *153 Fish* by Pamela Thibodeau Hardiman, St. Louis, Missouri, United States, for the Newman Center at the University of Massachusetts, Amherst. 1990. Panel measurements: 54″ x 24″ (137 x 61 cm). Cotton, tissue, lamé. Machine-piecing and quilting, hand-appliqué. When speaking of her impressive church work, Pamela says, "I am a quilter, so quilts are my medium...I felt starved of life and color in my (mostly) brick church, and I find that the softness of fabric and vivid color are perfect complements to the wood, brick, and stone of many church walls." She explains that the panels in figures 61b and 61c were commissioned by the Newman Center and depict the story from St. John's Gospel (John 21: 1-14) where the disciples of Jesus spend the night fishing unsuccessfully. As the sun rises, a figure appears on the shore and says, "Cast your net on the right side of the boat and you will find some." Lifting the net, the disciples find it filled to breaking point with 153 fish. St. Peter, recognizing the Lord, swims to meet Him, while Jesus awaits them on the shore with breakfast cooking. After the panels were delivered, Father C. Lee Gilbertson of the Newman Center commissioned a chasuble to go with them, and Pamela repeated the sea theme and her marvelous sparkling crosses to make a robe suitable for the "ordinary time" of the church year, when green vestments are worn. Father Gilbertson kindly modeled the chasuble for the photograph in figure 61a, which we chose for the cover of this book. Pamela made her first quilt at the age of twelve and says that her spirituality has grown with her art. You can see one of her quilts in figure 118. (Photographs courtesy Fred Moore)

62. *Road to Calvary* by Carol S. Riffe, Whitmore Lake, Milwaukee, United States, made for William Street United Methodist Church, Delaware, Ohio. 1990. 34″ x 80″ (86 x 203 cm). Cotton prints (some overdyed). Machine-pieced and quilted. American quilters have always given their patterns names, and many have a biblical reference. Carol Riffe chose three such blocks for her striking altar frontal—Hosanna, King's Cross, and Crown of Thorns—to represent the images of Holy Week. She then distorted the patterns so as to create a design with an unusual perspective. She used dark fabrics printed with birds and flowers to symbolize the Garden of Gethsemane (lower right) and cleverly evolved the Hosannah block to form abstract images of the three crosses on Calvary (top left). "The most important feature of the design is the illusion of light radiating from under the Crown of Thorns," Carol says. "This implies the person of Christ and alludes to the many places in Scripture where he is referred to as the 'Light of the World.'" She feels that people relate to quilt art at an emotional level; "perhaps there is a subliminal memory of the traditional quilt as shelter that evokes this response from people, so what could be more appropriate for church furnishings?" Her own church has a large collection of contemporary quilt art that includes pieces made by Carol, and this led to many commissions for her. (This particular frontal was commissioned as a memorial to a member of the William Street United Methodist Church.) (Photograph courtesy Jack Kenny)

63. *Festal Altar Frontal* designed and made by Deborah Melton Anderson, Columbus, Ohio, United States, for All Saints Evangelical Lutheran Church, Worthington, Ohio. 1987. Main frontal: 36″ x 71″ (91 x 180 cm). Raw silk, Thai silk, cotton duck. Machine-appliqué and reverse appliqué, machine-quilting. As an artist, Deborah Anderson says she loves to use fabrics to convey ideas appropriate to the liturgy. Her theme for this wonderfully textured piece is the Tree of Life into which she has ingeniously incorporated myriad Christian symbols. In the early days of Christianity, certain groups of letters derived from Greek or Latin words were used as symbols for Christ. For example, the monograms IC, XC, and XP (known as the Chi Rho; see fig. 2) that Deborah has worked on the main part of the frontal are either the first and last letters, or the first two letters, of the Greek words IHCOYC and XPICTOC meaning "Jesus" and "Christ," while the word NIKA (seen on the bottom right) is the Latin for "victor." She has also included a dove to symbolize the Holy Spirit; a bunch of grapes, a chalice, loaves of bread, and ears of wheat for the Eucharist; a fish that was one of the earliest symbols of Christianity; triangles to represent the Trinity; and the letters Alpha and Omega, meaning "the first" and "the last" that are taken from Revelations 1:8. Deborah is a member of the Liturgical Art Guild of Columbus that brings together architects, religious leaders, artists, and congregants to fulfill the liturgical needs of the community and has undertaken many commissions for both Christian and Jewish organizations. More of Deborah's work is illustrated in figures 116 and 117. (Photograph courtesy Noel Guitry)

64a, 64b, 64c. *Altar Frontal, Dean's Cope, and Transept Hangings.* Silk and cotton brocade, silver and gold-kid leather, gold braid, and semiprecious stones. Hand-appliqué and embroidery, also machine-embroidery. In 1977, a remarkable project, involving many members of the diocese, was undertaken at the Cathedral of Saint John the Evangelist in Spokane, Washington, U.S.A. This was to make hangings for the north and south transepts from designs left by the late cathedral architect, Harold Whitehouse. The cathedral authorities employed Eleanor Van de Water (whose work appears in figure 65) to prepare a timetable and budget, but the work was actually supervised by Dorothy Marsden who became known affectionately as "The Hanging Woman"! The designs called for appliqué and embroidered shields along the top edges of the hangings, so seventy ladies were invited to take part in a competition and were given sampler kits. It is a selection of these lovely competition samplers that you see forming the orphrey on the Dean's cope in figure 64b (modeled here by the verger, Tom Heal). This cope was also designed and made by a parishioner and has some fine machine-embroidery and appliqué on the back. Twenty-four ladies were finally chosen to embroider the shields for the transept hangings, and on some of them they used local stones that were collected and polished by a choir member who started as a choirboy in the old cathedral. The north transept hangings depict the emblems of the twelve apostles (fig. 64c), while on the south hanging the shields bear the arms of the eleven largest churches and the names of all the other churches in the diocese. This magnificent work was completed in time for the cathedral's fiftieth-anniversary celebration on October 19, 1979. (Photographs courtesy Dr. David C. Bunch, Spokane)

64c. Here you can see the emblem of the cathedral's patronal saint, Saint John the Evangelist. The gold chalice and a silver serpent refer to the legend where an attempt was made to murder Saint John by offering him a poisoned chalice. The intricate background design of couched gold braid was also worked by the parishioners. If this had been undertaken professionally, it would have cost $10,000!

65. *The Glory Frontal* made by Eleanor Van de Water, Vancouver, Washington, United States, for St. Bartholomew's Episcopal Parish Church. 1991. Two panels 36″ x 144″ (92 x 366 cm). Each embellished portion 36″ x 48″ (92 x 122 cm). Raw silk, gold, silver and copper leather and lamé, cords. Hand-appliqué with some trapunto. This beautiful frontal is aptly named and is one of a set made to commemorate the twenty-fifth anniversary of the construction of St. Bartholomew's Church in Beaverton, Oregon. As the frontal was to be used on a central altar, Eleanor made it in two separate panels that are placed on the altar in the form of a cross, but she embellished only those parts that cover the front and the sides with her glittering appliqué. "My intent was to express the exhilaration and joy of Christmas and of Easter—the visual statement of the words 'Thine is the kingdom and the power and the *glory*,'" she explains. Although she is self-taught, Eleanor has been working professionally for twenty-five years, mostly in the liturgical field. "I feel very clearly that I have found a purpose for my life. Working with various denominations has helped me to clarify my own faith and has broadened my understanding and appreciation of individual needs and differences." She used fusible interfacing (Wonder-Under) to bond the lamé fabrics and covered the raw edges with couched cords. The padded portions were finished by turning the edges under and blind-stitching them to the background. (Photograph courtesy the artist)

66a, 66b, 66c, 66d. *Holy Spirit Chasuble* by Sister Josephine Niemann, S.S.N.D., St. Louis, Missouri, United States. 1990. Polyester. Machine-piecing. Sister Josephine is a Catholic nun and a member of the School Sisters of Notre Dame. "We have had an ecclesiastical department in our motherhouse here in St. Louis for almost one hundred years," she explains. "When I developed asthma in 1982, I decided that it was time to stop teaching and become a full-time artist." (She taught art in secondary schools for over twenty years, most recently in Sierra Leone, Africa.) After trying many different kinds of art, in the end it was liturgical work that seemed to beckon. Now eighty percent of her work is in this field, and much of it involves quilting techniques because she comes from a family where quiltmaking has been a tradition for more than five generations. For this fascinating chasuble that is used at Pentecost and for confirmation services (figs. 66a, 66b), Sister Josephine wanted an unrepresentational design that suggested the Holy Spirit. "I wanted to convey movement and an illusion of wind," she says. She was certainly successful, for the robe gives a wonderful sense of a bird in flight. Sister Josephine works with ten other sisters from the order and in figures 66c and 66d you can see two of her banners. (Photographs courtesy John Wm. Nagel, Webster Groves, Missouri)

66c. *Processional Banner for St. Louis Cathedral.* 360″ x 34″ (916 x 86.4 cm). Nylon mosquito netting, gold metallic fabric, nylon fabric, satin ribbons. This is one of six processional banners made by Sister Josephine for the ordination ceremony of Bishop Paul Zipfel in St. Louis Cathedral in 1989, and she based her design on a medieval military standard. "Because they can be held high, the banners can easily be seen by worshippers anywhere in the cathedral." The method of construction is ingenious. The appliqué cross is mounted on mosquito netting that allows the air to flow through it so there is almost no wind resistance. The frame is made from PVC tubing covered in gold fabric that slots into an aluminum shower rod. The long ribbons are attached with velcro for easy removal and storage. (Photograph courtesy the artist)

66d. In 1988, Sister Josephine was asked by the Archdiocese of Seattle to design a rite-of-committal banner for the Associated Catholic Cemeteries. The banner measures 360″ x 42″ (916 x 107 cm) and when she thought about the mourners at a funeral and the need for comfort, Sister Josephine says, "I was convinced that the softness of a quilt was what was needed." Unfortunately, Seattle has a rainy climate and because it was used outside, the machine-pieced and quilted banner proved impractical, so a year later Sister Josephine made a replacement in nylon fabric without batting or lining. She borrowed part of the design from a quilt by Pamela Hardiman, whose work appears in figures 62a, 62b, 62c, and 118. "I did not know her at the time, and we became friends later, but I recognized her cross (see figure 118) as a wonderful symbol of the glorified Christ." (Photographs courtesy the artist and Associated Catholic Cemeteries, Seattle)

67a, 67b. *Two Stoles* made by Judy B. Dales, Boonton, New Jersey, United States, for Dr. Larry Kalp and Val Pedersen of the United Church of Christ (the "Community Church"), Mountain Lakes, New Jersey. 1990 and 1991. Cottons (some hand-dyed). Hand-pieced. Judy is a professional quilter, and as she travels throughout the United States and abroad teaching and lecturing, she says that she does not have time to do traditional volunteer work, so she is pleased to be able to use her quilting talents for church work. She made the beautifully worked stole in figure 67a for Dr. Larry Kalp (who wears it in the photograph) to commemorate his installation as the pastor of her church. "I have done a lot of curved seam work in the past five years so the graceful, flowing lines seemed right for a stole. The symbols were chosen by Dr. Kalp and include flames for purity (Pentecost); the descending dove to represent the Holy Spirit; water for Baptism; the Star of Bethlehem, and a chalice, which you can just see as a faint silhouette behind the star. "It was a challenge to arrange so many symbols in one small stole!" Judy says, "and I added the cross on the upper right to balance the heaviness of the dove." Judy made the second stole for Val Pedersen, music director at the church (fig. 67b). "I felt that Val's job is a musical ministry, so she should have a stole just like our other ministers. The descending dove and the flowing curves represent the spiritual peace that music brings to worship." (Photographs courtesy the artist)

68a, 68b, 68c, 68d. *Creation Chasuble and Stole* by Colleen L. Hintz, Sparta, New Jersey, United States, for the Episcopal Church of the Redeemer, Morristown, New Jersey. 1990. Cottons, hand-painted silk leaves by Krista O'Brien. Machine appliqué, hand embroidery. This delightful set of vestments was designed by Colleen for the Reverend Phillip D. Wilson (who is seen here wearing them) for "The Season of Creation." This is a special season conceived by the rector that takes place during the latter part of Pentecost to celebrate and encourage stewardship of the earth, and which uses earth tones for the liturgical color. The chasuble was also made as a memorial to Eric Johnson, who was closely associated with the church until his tragic death from AIDS at the age of thirty-two. The church now has an active AIDS ministry. Colleen chose the grapevine because of its symbolism (see John 15:5) and to illustrate the cycle of life. "The vine starts on the front of the robe and then moves to the back where the leaves grow bigger and the fruit comes into fullness. Gradually, the leaves turn brown, the fruit withers and we return to the front of the robe again where a single leaf, full of holes, falls to the ground to bring nourishment to life that will come again." As she worked on the chasuble, Colleen felt the design represented Eric's life. "He was the leaf that fell to the ground, but he was also the fullness of the fruit in the church's AIDS ministry." The design for the charming "Creation" stole centers on locally known images of God's creation. "Jack-in-the-Pulpit" with its bright red berries is a familiar Fall image, and the milkweed pod with its seeds scattering in the wind is the hope of life continuing (fig 68c). The hibernating chipmunk in figure 68d is a favorite image of Colleen's daughter. Colleen says that the concept of God, the Creator, has taken on new meaning for her since she began designing liturgical art. (Photographs courtesy M. Patrick Hintz)

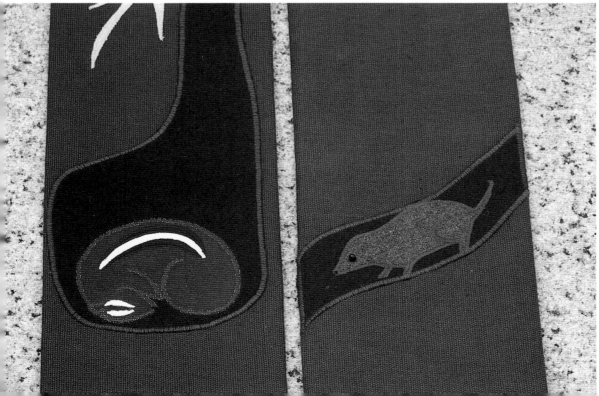

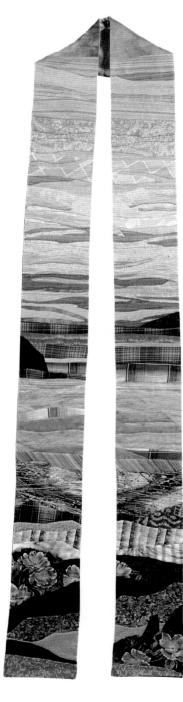

69a, 69b. *Maine Isle Morn and Ieradi Stole* by Susan K. Turbak, Cambridge, Massachusetts, United States. 1980 and 1989. Hanging: 78″ x 40″ (198 x 101.6 cm). Cottons, cotton blends. Hand-appliqué and quilting. Susan sees sunrises as God's way of acknowledging our existence and giving us another day to find out what we are supposed to be doing with our lives and the world we live in. She explains, "It was after spending two weeks on Duck Island, off the coast of Maine, that I came home, quit my office job, and started creating *Maine Isle Morn*, and my life took a completely different direction." (A well-known quiltmaker, she now works in the Massachusetts Institute of Technology in the Earth Resources Laboratory.) Although this lovely, tranquil piece was not made for a specific church, it was considered to be spiritually appropriate for church settings. The worship committees of the Church of the Covenant in Boston and Old Cambridge Baptist Church have both hung it for several years running either during Lent, or for Easter Sunday and the Easter season. In 1989, when Susan was commissioned by Old Cambridge Baptist Church to make a stole as a gift for Ann Ieradi on her ordination, she once again took a sunrise as her theme (fig. 69b). "Ann was called to minister to a church in Carver, Massachusetts, which is near the ocean, and I was asked to represent the area. In talking with her, I found that Ann also had a strong attachment to the rising and the setting of the sun, but I felt that the paler colors of the sunrise fitted her personality and the type of ministry I had witnessed from her." Another of Susan's superb landscape quilts appears in figure 69c. (Photographs courtesy David Caras)

69c. *Psalm 95:4* by Susan K. Turbak, Cambridge, Massachusetts, United States. 1985. 95″ x 75″ (241.3 x 190.5 cm). Cottons, cotton blends, fiberglass. Hand-appliqué and quilting. For the past thirteen years Susan has been combining her deep love of nature and of working with color and fabric by creating landscapes with appliqué (see figs. 69a, 69b). She teaches and lectures on quiltmaking and says that she believes that her ability to create landscapes is a gift from God. "Whenever possible, I acknowledge that in my work either by presenting my view of His creation in nature, or by title, or through teaching others how to observe color and form and encouraging them to explore their own creativity." This striking piece was inspired by a verse from one of Susan's favorite psalms, "In God's hands are the depths of the earth, the rocks and the hills are also his." She explains that the scene is not of any particular place "but celebrates the time of year just before the trees bud, when the mountains are thawing and the streams run swiftly." Like *Maine Isle Morn*, this quilt has also been borrowed for many years by the Old Cambridge Baptist Church for their Pentecost service and for the month following. (Photograph courtesy David Caras)

70a. *Josephina* designed and made by Linda Fowler, Columbus, Ohio, United States, for St. Turibius Chapel in the Pontifical College Josephinum, Columbus. 1989. 96″ x 72″ (244 x 183 cm). Cotton and cotton blends. Machine-pieced, hand-quilted. Linda manages to combine sacred, secular, and personal themes in her remarkable quilted wall-hangings. She spent twenty-eight years in religious life (she was a member of the Sisters of St. Joseph in Columbus), but her travels to Spain, Greece, Turkey, and Egypt, and the artistic excitement she finds in color, pattern, composition, and texture all contribute to the wonderful vitality of her work. She likes to include arches, doorways, stairways, and other architectural elements to create illusions of space and perspective. "Much of my work is based on the Christian form of the arch," she says. "I have made numerous quilts with portals suggesting entry and movement along our spiritual journey of life." The inspiration for this stunning hanging came from the arches in St. Turibius chapel (where it now hangs) and the stairway to the choir loft. "My idea was to depict the church as a boat related to and built on the past, but sailing into the future on the waters of life." Because she wanted to combine her sewing skills and her fine-arts background to serve the church, Linda now makes hangings and vestments on a full-time basis, assisted by her mother, Viva Fowler. Another of her hangings appears in figure 70b. (Photographs courtesy the artist)

70b. *In Paradisium I* made by Linda Fowler as a memorial to Father Eugene Yoris for the Liturgical Art Guild of Ohio. 1990. 36½″ x 35″ (92.7 x 88.9 cm). Cottons and cotton blends. Machine-pieced, hand-quilted. This quilt is part of the Liturgical Guild's traveling collection that goes out to member churches. The design was inspired by Gabriel Fauré's requiem "May the Angels Lead You into Paradise," which was played at Father Yoris's funeral, so Linda included a palm tree, a symbol of paradise, and an arch as a symbol of heaven.

71. *John 14:27* by Donna Duchesne Garofalo, North Windham, Connecticut, United States, for Chaplin Congregational Church, Connecticut. 1987. 60″ x 40″ (152.4 x 101.6 cm). Cottons, cotton blends, silver lamé. Machine-piecing, hand-appliqué, and quilting. When the new wing for the Sunday school was completed at Chaplin Congregational Church, Donna was asked to hang some of her quilted wall-hangings in the fellowship hall, and she made this lovely tranquil piece as a gift. "I prayerfully decided that I would depict the coming of the Holy spirit," she explains. "I gave the hanging the title of John 14:27 because of the beautiful promise Jesus gives us in this passage. He tells us in verse 26 that 'the Holy Spirit, whom the Father will send in my name, will teach you all things,' and in verse 27 He says 'Peace I leave with you; my peace I give you. I do not give it to you as the world gives. Do not let your hearts be troubled and do not be afraid.' What powerful and comforting words! I hope that all who look at my hanging will be reminded of this promise and of the work of the Holy Spirit." As an artist, Donna has been using quilting techniques for ten years. She finds fabric a challenging and absorbing medium. Solving construction problems and making her design work in fabric is both stimulating and rewarding, but she adds, "My love and respect for God's creation and its beauty play an important part in my designing. I consider my abilities to be a gift from Him." (Photograph courtesy Jeff Burnham)

72. *The Parable of the Seed* by Joanne Kost, Sandy Hook, Connecticut, United States, for the First Evangelical Free Church, Rockford, Illinois. 1987. 96″ x 96″ (244 x 244 cm). Cotton, cotton blends. Hand-appliqué and quilting, some machine-piecing. This stunning triptych was made as a memorial to Phyllis Nelson, who had been a member of the congregation of the First Free Evangelical Church and an avid quilter during her lifetime. When Joanne received the commission, she asked the Nelson family to supply a text from the Bible from which she could draw inspiration. They chose the Parable of the Sower from Matthew 13:3-23. "I decided to make my interpretation fairly literal because there were so many visual elements in the text," Joanne explains. "I was nervous at attempting such a large project (the size was determined by the area in which it was to hang), but when I had finished it and stepped back to look, there was a great feeling of joy and accomplishment. I had an awesome feeling of having been divinely guided." Her design reads as follows, *left panel:* "As he was scattering the seed, some fell on the path, and the birds ate it up. *Along the bottom edge of the hanging:* "Some fell on rocky places, where it did not have much soil... But when the sun came up... the plants withered because they had no root." *Right panel:* "Other seed fell among thistles which grew up and choked the plant." *Main panel:* "Some found good soil and bore fruit." Joanne's work is well-known to quilters all over the world from *Quilter's Newsletter Magazine*, which published this photograph in April 1989. Joanne says that she has always found inspiration in words, particularly words from the Bible, and you can see another of her biblically inspired quilts in figure 119. (Photograph courtesy Bob Kost)

73. *Trinity* by Margaret Hays, Mill Creek, Washington, United States, for Trinity Church, Portland, Oregon. 1975. 76″ x 41″ (193 x 104 cm). Silk, satin, brocade, metallic fabric, taffeta. Hand-applique and quilting. This portrayal of the Trinity, showing God the Father as an elderly man wearing a crown, supporting his Son on a cross upon His knees, with a descending dove as the Holy Spirit, is often seen in medieval art, and the inspiration for this striking piece was actually taken from an illuminated manuscript. It is one of Margaret Hays's favorite ways of presenting this complex image. Some years previously, she had shown a similar hanging at a meeting at Trinity Church, so when the church was "un-remodeled" (i.e. returned to the state of its original design of the late 1800s), the priest requested a new version for a niche beside the altar. Margaret trained as a sculptor and she thinks of her work as a form of fabric relief. She works in layers, constructing the background just like a quilt with a backing, batting, and a top fabric. The figures and motifs are also layered and then applied to the background, so that the depth, particularly in large pieces, can be as much as three or four inches. She mounts the finished work on heavy canvas that acts as a support and prevents sagging, and which also forces the sculptural form forward. "I guess I became a quilter by the back door because I have never made a quilt for a bed. I have been using this technique for seventeen years and I don't know anyone who works in quite the same manner as I do." Two more of her beautiful pieces are illustrated in figures 120 and 121. (Photograph courtesy Richard E. Hays)

74a, 74b. *Flaming Chalice* made by Betty Deane, Eastham, Massachusetts, United States, for the First Parish Brewster ("The Church of the Sea Captains"), Brewster. 72″ x 48″ (182.8 x 122 cm). Cotton and cotton blends. Hand-appliqué and quilting. In 1982, Betty Deane decided to make a permanent banner to hang behind the pulpit of her local church to commemorate the installation of the Reverend James Robinson. The church is known as "the Church of the Sea Captains" because of its association with the sailing vessels of the past. You can see the paintings of these great ships in figure 74b. Betty explains that she wanted to make something meaningful, "so what better than the logo of our denomination. The church is Unitarian and Universalist, so the two circles represent the merger of the two religions while the flaming chalice, in the words of Pastor Robinson, 'symbolizes the religious values that we cherish: love, truth, compassion, service, justice, peace.'" The banner was made in time for the installation, but not quilted. "Some people said that it looked good the way it was," Betty says, but she insisted on quilting it by hand as a tribute to the wives of the old sea captains. "I felt they probably quilted while they waited for their husbands to return—it was an art and need of their time." The banner was finally finished in February 1985 and is a memorial to the women "who came before us and to their talents which have enriched our lives and our faith." (Photographs courtesy Richard S. Furbush [banner] and Charles N. Deane [interior of church])

75a, 75b. *Resurrection and Epiphany Banners* designed by Barbara Rickey, Bellevue, Washington, United States, and made by the Eastgate Quilters for the Eastgate Congregational United Church of Christ, Bellevue. 1987. 48″ x 48″ (122 x 122 cm) and 41″ x 33″ (104 x 84 cm). Polished cotton, linen, satin, silk, gold lamé. Machine-appliqué, hand-quilting. In 1985, after more than ten years of quiltmaking, the women's fellowship sewing group at Eastgate Church decided to make a series of seasonal wall-hangings to be displayed in turn in the narthex. These two attractive hangings are part of the series that was completed in 1989. *Resurrection* (fig. 75a) is hung at Eastertide and depicts the cross fleurée, so named because of the fleur-de-lys at the end of each cross-bar. The four small crosses represent the message of the Gospel spreading to the four corners of the earth. Barbara Rickey explains that they "used gold fabric for the crosses because the Resurrection changed the wooden cross into something untarnishable and everlasting. The butterfly, and the lily that we quilted in the outer corners, are also traditional symbols of the Resurrection." Pastor Dr. John C. Randlett suggested the symbols of *Epiphany* (fig. 75b). "The Crown of Life that God promised to all those who love Him symbolizes the Kingship of Our Lord and is also part of our church's logo. The curved lines are the living water referred to in St. John's Gospel (see John 4:14) and also represent baptism, while Alleluia is our response to the proclamation of the good news of great joy to all people." The next major project of the Eastgate Quilters is a group of banners for the sanctuary. (Photographs courtesy Barbara Rickey)

76a. *The Banners of Christ* designed by William R. Phinnie for St. Paul's Episcopal Church, Kilgore, Texas, United States. 1991. 36″ x 30″ (91.4 x 76.2 cm). Mr. and Mrs. Paul M. Branch of Kilgore, Texas, are keen travelers and having been impressed by the sight of the medieval banners hanging in the great cathedrals and abbeys of England, they commissioned William R. Phinnie to make eight banners to hang from the rafters of their church. They gave Bill Phinnie complete freedom to choose the designs, and he explains that he chose "the animal and botanical symbols of Christ's Passion and Resurrection because many of them are familiar from early Christian times. Just as the letters of the alphabet are symbols of our language, so Christian symbols are the language of our faith, and we must learn not merely to look at the symbols but to look through them to the truths that they express." Each banner has a different type of cross on the back. In order to find needlewomen capable of interpreting his designs, Bill first of all contacted Connie Brooks from Bullard who had done some fine needlework for a church in the vicinity, and as extra help was needed he then got in touch with the Dallas Needlework and Textile Guild (a branch of the Embroiderers' Guild of America). Jeanette Conrad from Bedford and Judith Logan from Dallas applied, and all three ladies worked closely with Bill throughout the duration of this magnificent project. Jeanette is now working on an "afterthought," a processional banner in similar style. (Photographs courtesy Lori Knuth)

76b. *The Pelican-in-her-Piety* worked by Connie Brooks and Jeanette Conrad. Silk-damask white *peau-de-soie* for the bird's body, satin, glass beads, gold-kid leather, cord, jewel stones. Hand-appliqué and embroidery, trapunto. From the thirteenth century, the pelican has been widely used as a symbol of Christ the Redeemer. In medieval times naturalists believed that in times of famine the pelican would pluck her own breast and feed her chicks with her life-blood. The passion-flower as a symbol is believed to have come from the early Spanish settlers in America who used it to illustrate Christ's passion to the Indians because within its blossom you can see a hammer, the nails, the wounds, a nimbus, and a spear. The banner is dedicated to the Reverend Jacquelin Washington and the reverse side has an anchor cross symbolizing hope.

76c. *The Peacock* worked by Jeanette Conrad and Judith Logan. Silk-damask, white Ultrasuede for the body, blue and green metallic fabric, metallic net, sequins, glass stones, Ultrasuede (grapes and leaves), gold-kid leather, and gold bugle beads (wheat). Hand-appliqué and embroidery, trapunto. To construct the lovely peacock's tail, Jeanette made the feathers from two layers of shimmering fabric sandwiched together with fusible interfacing and overlaid with metallic net. The peacock is an ancient symbol for Christ's Resurrection and immortality, as seen in the annual shedding and replacement of the bird's plumage. Wheat and grapes are a symbol of the Eucharist. This banner is dedicated to Lillian Margaret Landes and on the reverse has a silver cross/sword piercing a winged heart.

76d, 76e. *The Cock of Christian Vigilance* worked by Jeanette Conrad and Judith Logan. Silk-damask, applied sequins, gold- and silver-kid leather, cord, beads. Hand-appliqué, trapunto, and embroidery. The tail, body, and head of this beautiful sequin cock were worked by Jeanette on separate pieces of fabric and then applied. The cock and the cross keys are the symbols of St. Peter, but the design also symbolizes the vigil of Christ in Gethsemane. "The stars and the quarter moon denote the night watch of sorrow." The banner is dedicated to William M. Routon, Jr., and on the back it has the keys and the reversed cross on which, according to legend, St. Peter was crucified upside-down as he felt unworthy to die in the same position as his Master.

77a, 77b. *Easter Lily and Advent Banners* made by Gerry Enger, Wappinger Falls, New York, United States, for Grace United Methodist Church, Lindenhurst, New York. 1990. Cottons, fur fabric. Cathedral Window piecing, machine-piecing, hand-appliqué, and quilting. When Gerry attended a religious retreat in 1989, a stranger turned and said to her, "It doesn't matter how far away you must go, God has work for you to do." Soon afterward, she decided to attend Grace Methodist Church that was some distance from her home, and as a needlewoman of long standing, she began to have visions of banners that she wanted to make for her new church. This charming Easter Lily banner was the first one Gerry made. The original border design came from a course she attended on creative quilting, where the assignment was to "close your eyes and scribble." When Gerry reflected her "scribble" in a mirror, she found that she had drawn half of an Easter lily. "I never knew how to use the design until I joined Grace Church, and then I saw it as part of a banner." One of Gerry's favorite Christmas hymns is "Come All Ye Faithful" and when designing the richly colored Advent banner (fig. 77b), she tried to incorporate all the visual images from this hymn. "I wanted it to remind people of a medieval tapestry," she says. "So I chose the colors accordingly." The inspiration for the Cathedral Window border came from the wooden carving on the pulpit. The machine-pieced star, which is made up of more than sixty pieces, reflects a phrase from the hymn "Light from Light Eternal." Gerry has been interested in needlework ever since the first grade and now works as a folk artist. She also teaches quiltmaking to Grace Church members. (Photograph courtesy Brant Brown, East Islip, New York)

78. *Love So Amazing* designed by Robert Plouffe and made by Esther R. Jackson, Warwick, Rhode Island, United States, for Greenwood Presbyterian Community Church. 1982. 48″ x 48″ (122 x 122 cm). Cottons. Hand-appliqué. The stained-glass technique is used to great effect in this dramatic banner depicting well-known Christian symbols. Esther Jackson made it originally for Greenwood Presbyterian Community Church to take to the General Assembly of the Presbyterian Church U.S.A. at Hartford, Connecticut, in 1982. The theme of the assembly was "Love So Amazing," and the original idea for the design came from the pastor of Greenwood Church, Dr. Robert Peterson. Esther's contribution was the coloring and the method of construction. The letters flanking the simple cross are Alpha and Omega, the first and last letters of the Greek alphabet that are often used as a designation for both God and Christ (see Revelations 1:8). Esther was worried that after the Assembly was over, the banner would not have a home, but it now hangs in the new addition to Greenwood Church. Esther has been teaching quilting and rug-hooking at adult community programs and at home for about thirty years. "I enjoy the fellowship of crafts people," she says. "You learn so much, but my friendships at my church group have always been the center of my life." (Photograph courtesy Richard Arling of Arling Studio)

79a, 79b. *Holy Spirit/Great Spirit* designed by Louise Leonard and made by members of the congregation for The Holy Family Cathedral, Anchorage, Alaska, United States. 1986. 180″ x 60″ (458 x 152 cm). Cottons. Hand-appliqué and beading. When Louise was asked to design a banner to hang in the Holy Family Cathedral, she decided to do it in the style of the wooden dance masks traditionally used by Alaskans to portray the Great Spirit. She describes the spirituality that inspired her design. "Our grandmothers and grandfathers taught us a sense of awareness of every blade of grass, of every fish. Living of life isn't just between you and me, or me and the grass, it is all in relation to the person of the universe. The eye of the universe is aware of everything, so we're all part of a connection. You and the sunset are not just you and the sunset...you have respect for everything. The symbols are examples of all earth....Everything has a spirit... so everything has connection with the person of the universe." In figure 79b you can see the group working on the banner. Seated left to right: Rebecca Amarak, Helen Pushruk, Angela Newman, (unidentified), Daisy Demientieff, Louise Leonard, Mary Catherine Talley, Agnes Mayac. Standing behind: Margaret Tochavik, Marie Tyson, Katherine Manook, Christina Casica, and Sister Kevin Flynn, S.L.C. The fact that their work is being featured in a book has brought these ladies together again, and they are now enthusiastically thinking about another project. (Photographs courtesy the Archdiocese of Anchorage)

80. *275th Anniversary Quilt* designed by Dorothy Sime, Pembroke, Massachusetts, United States, and made by members of the congregation of the First Church in Pembroke. 1987. 96″ x 72″ (244 x 183 cm). Cottons. Machine- and hand-piecing. Hand-appliqué and quilting. This charming banner was made to commemorate the 275th anniversary of the founding of the First Church in Pembroke, and each block was carefully thought out to symbolize an event in the church's year and to illustrate a text from the Bible. The original design and the center medallion depicting the church were the work of Dorothy Sime, based on a drawing by Mary Ann Simmons. The church depicted is not the original building; the present church was built in 1839. Dorothy was the only experienced quilter in the group, so before the project began she gave the other sixteen ladies quilting lessons. The banner now hangs in the parish hall, and Dorothy says of her design that "the church is the focal point of the quilt, just as it is the focus of all of us who worked on the project." The symbolism of each block is explained as follows: Starting top left: *Advent Candles*, John 1:9, made by Lynn Perekslis; *Mother and Child*, Luke 2:11, made by Gail Sim; *Bethlehem*, Luke 2:11, made by Pat Schjolden; *Epiphany Star*, Matthew 2:10, made by Ann McKinnon; *Cross and Crown*, Luke 18: 32-33, made by Marilyn Levandoski; *Hosannah!*, Luke 19:38, made by Lois Roberts; *Wheat*, John 12:24, made by Laurie DeCoste; *Shells*, Ephesians 4: 5-6, made by Peggy O'Neil Files; *Communion Paten*, Luke 22:19, made by Dorothy Sime and Sue Hewitt; *Boat*, Matthew 28:19, made by Gail Sim; *Chalice*, Luke 22:20, made by Sue Hewitt; *Grapes*, John 15:5, made by Lois Roberts; *Root of Jesse*, Isaiah 11:1, made by Marilyn Levandoski and Everlyn Orcutt; *Easter Sunrise*, Mark 16:2, made by Gail Jones; *Easter Lily*, 1 Corinthians 15:14, made by Helen Healey; *Victory Banner*, 1 Corinthians 15:57, made by Laurie DeCoste; *Dove*, Luke 3:22, made by Jan Burke Johnson; *Pentecostal Cross*, Acts 2:17, made by Jan King; *Bible and Sword*, 1 Peter 1:25, made by Gail Sim and Ann McKinnon; *United Church of Christ Symbol*, Romans 16:16, made by Nancy Steele; *Jacob's Ladder*, Genesis 28:22, made by Nancy Steele. (Photograph courtesy Bruce Orcutt)

Canada

81a, 81b. *Renewal* by Elizabeth Taylor, London, Ontario, Canada, for St. Paul's Cathedral, London. 1988. 48″ x 36″ x 60″ (122 x 92 x 153 cm). Silk. Machine-piecing, hand-appliqué and embroidery, hand-quilted by the ladies of the cathedral. This striking contemporary altar frontal is four-sided and when it was entered with the matching burse and veil for the Liturgical Arts Festival in Toronto in 1989, it won the "Best of Show" award. St. Paul's Cathedral commissioned the piece from Elizabeth, who is a well-known Canadian fiber artist, and gave her "renewal" as a theme. Elizabeth explains that as the altar has four sides, the birth and death of the year through the four seasons seemed appropriate. She took her inspiration from the Book of Job 14: 7-9. "At least there is hope for a tree: If it is cut down, it will sprout again, and its new shoots will not fail. Its roots may grow old in the ground and its stump die in the soil, yet at the scent of water it will bud and put forth shoots like a plant." Figure 81a shows the Autumn face of the frontal, while figure 81b depicts the Summer side. Elizabeth loves her ecclesiastical work. "It seems to be something that God has led me to do and I feel very privileged to be able to serve Him in a way that is such fun and so exciting." She says that she enjoys the challenge of "matching" a design to the church. "So often modern pieces don't seem to connect in any way to the building they inhabit, but designs can be contemporary and complement any type of architecture. This 'matching' leads to a refreshing variety of pieces." Elizabeth says her work divides neatly between commissioned ecclesiastical work and "personal" pieces that she sells through shows. (Photographs courtesy the artist)

82a, 82b, 82c. *Celtic Communion Table Cover and Lectern Fall* by Elma Kramers; *Lectern Fall* by Joyce Harris; of Ottawa and Nepean, Ontario, Canada, for Knox Presbyterian Church, Ottawa. 1992. Table cover, 8″ x 91″ x 30″ (20 x 231 x 76.2 cm). Lectern falls 22″ x 18″ (55.8 x 45.7 cm). Cotton, polyester, satin, linen, raw silk, viscose. Hand-appliqué and quilting. In spite of having two magnificent stained-glass windows, the interior of Knox Church is dark because it is built of the local gray sandstone. Seven years ago, two members of the congregation, Elma Kramers and Joyce Harris, decided to make new furnishings in the four liturgical colors of white, red, purple, and green in order to introduce some much-needed color. The designs of each set vary, but for her handsome green set (figs. 82a, 82b), Elma was attracted by Celtic interlace "because it has no beginning and no end. It is therefore symbolic of the eternal significance of the Cross. Also, Celtic designs are usually thought of as being of Scottish origin, which fits in well with the Presbyterian tradition." The ship on Joyce's charming lectern fall in figure 82c is often used as a symbol for the Christian church venturing on the sea of life. Now both ladies are thinking about making some quilted wall-hangings for the church. (Photographs courtesy Michael Bowie)

83. *Quilted Altar Frontal* designed by the late Ruth Plomer and Marion Hardy, Niagara-on-the-Lake, Ontario, Canada, for St. George's Anglican Church, Homer, Ontario. 1986. 38″ x 48″ (96.5 x 122 cm). Cotton blend, polyester satin. Hand-appliqué, embroidery, and quilting. (Alexa Millet and Mary Ellis from St. George's Church assisted with the quilting.) Marion Hardy, the designer of this elegant frontal says that she became a quilter about ten years ago. "I was going to church midweek, and I saw a group of ladies going into the Parish Hall carrying bags of fabric. Being a nosy person, I went over and found they were holding a series of quilting workshops. I asked if I could sign up, and this was the beginning of a new life for me!" The two panels on each side of the cross of St. George, the patron saint of the church, are quilted with grapevines, symbolic not only of the Eucharist but also of the many vineyards in the Niagara area. The little medallion in the center bears the sacred monogram IHS, which is derived from the Greek word IHCOYC, meaning Jesus. (Photograph courtesy Kenneth W. Hill, Niagara-on-the-Lake)

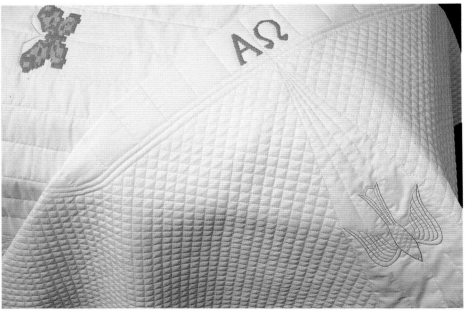

84a, 84b. *Quilted Funeral Pall* designed by Marion Hardy and Maggie Hammerling, Niagara-on-the-Lake, Ontario, Canada, for St. Mark's Anglican Church. 1990. (Assisted by Mary Ellis, Alina Millet, Joyce Brinsmead and Ellen Lea.) 92″ x 144″ (234 x 366 cm). Cotton, hand-embroidered, and quilted. Funeral palls are a necessary part of church regalia, and in this finely worked piece the two designers settled for the simple beauty of pure white and enlivened it with touches of gold embroidery. On the top in the center they placed a Jerusalem cross (the five crosses represent the five wounds of Christ) flanked by two butterflies, symbols of the Resurrection. In figure 84b is illustrated a dove symbolizing the Holy Spirit that they embroidered on each corner of the pall and the Greek letters, Alpha and Omega. These photographs appeared in a book *Ontario's Heritage Quilts* by Marilyn I. Walker, and they are reproduced with the author's permission.

85. *Festival Frontal* designed by Nancy-Lou Patterson, Waterloo, Ontario, Canada, for All Saints Anglican Church, Waterloo, and made by members of the parish. 1988. 36½″ x 77″ (92.7 x 195.5 cm). Cotton blends. Machine-pieced, hand-appliqué, and quilting. Nancy-Lou Patterson, a Professor of Fine Art at the University of Waterloo, is one of Canada's foremost liturgical artists. She has collected Mennonite quilts for some thirty years, and the account of how she used Mennonite quilters to make an enormous hanging for another church in Ontario appears in the caption for figure 1. She says that because the hanging *Feed My Sheep* proved so successful, she began designing pieces for other groups to make, of which this superb altar frontal is one. Twenty-nine ladies from the parish of All Saints took part. "All Saints shares its building with a Presbyterian church, and the Anglicans needed a frontal that they could whisk off the altar quickly in order to leave it unadorned for the more austere requirements of the Presbyterians," Nancy-Lou explains. "The design represents an image of Paradise, based upon the Tree of Knowledge in Genesis 2:9 and Revelations 22:2. The two trees, placed on each side of a mandala-shaped image containing the Cross, are flanked by the sun and the moon as cosmic witnesses to the Incarnation, the Crucifixion, and the Resurrection. Pieced stars witness the events from above, while the earth below sprouts lilies (symbols of the Annunciation), roses (symbols of Mary and Jesus), and crocuses (symbols of the resurrection of the dead and the Resurrection of Jesus)." The image of Paradise has a special significance for Nancy-Lou because it is a primary source of symbolism in Mennonite folk art. More of Nancy-Lou's fascinating work can be seen in figures 86 and 87. (Photograph courtesy the artist)

86. *Our Lady of Israel* designed and made by Nancy-Lou Patterson, Waterloo, Ontario, Canada, for St. George-Forest Hill Anglican Church, Kitchener. 1981. 72″ x 34″ (182.8 x 86.3 cm). Cotton blends. Hand-appliqué and embroidery. This beautiful hanging was commissioned by a family from St. George's to commemorate their adoption of two Asian "boat" children, and it now hangs beside the font. "In 1979, my husband and I visited the Nass Valley in British Columbia where the Nishga, one of the great First Nations, live. I drove on a logging road over two ranges of mountains to reach this remote and sublimely beautiful place. The Nishga are, to a large extent, Anglicans and worshipping with them was an overwhelming experience. All the images from this area, the mountains, the waterfalls, and the forest are in my design. My home is in some of the richest farmland in Canada in southern Ontario, so I included the fields and wildflowers from this region too. I depicted Our Lady and her Son as Asians, or native people, in honor of the children adopted by the family who commissioned the banner and of the native people of Canada....Jesus became incarnate of His mother, taking the entire creation upon Himself with her flesh, therefore I have girded Our Lady as an embodiment of the earth with a background of sky and stars representing the cosmos. Above her head is the *Tetragrammaton*, the divine name of God in Hebrew. On the breast of the Christ Child is his sacred heart." Nancy-Lou explains that the Anglican church is "the well-spring" of her art, religious or secular. She works in other media, including illustration. (Photograph courtesy the artist)

87. *Pentecost Banner* designed by Nancy-Lou Patterson, Waterloo, Ontario, Canada; pieced by Patricia MacLean and quilted by Marjorie Heimbach for St. Columba's Church, Waterloo. 1983. 72″ x 36″ (182.8 x 91.4 cm). Cotton blends. Machine-pieced, hand-quilted. Nancy-Lou is a trained artist, and although she has raised nine children and now has six grandchildren, she has never thought of herself as a housewife (she has been a university teacher nearly all her adult life), but she enjoys using a traditional woman's art like quiltmaking to express liturgical symbols in contemporary terms. When other people are involved, she says, "It is easy to explain what you want them to do because so many people already know how to make quilts. The validation of the work of women (my own included) for the most sacred of places appeals to me mightily." Nancy-Lou has designed a number of pieces for groups to make (see fig. 85). In this wonderfully graphic piece, she uses patchwork to depict symbols associated with the Holy Spirit and Pentecost. "The yellow in the upper part of the hanging symbolizes light; the white dove with the seven red flames symbolizes the Holy Spirit and the flames of Pentecost, and the seven sacraments; the blue areas represent water; the whitish areas signify air (wind), while the green area at the base is the earth. Thus we have the four elements, fire, water, air, and earth out of which, with the addition of light, God created the universe. All are symbols of the action of the Holy Spirit, who brooded over the waters of Creation, the Incarnation of Jesus, and the inspiration of the Apostles at the first Pentecost." (Photograph courtesy the artist)

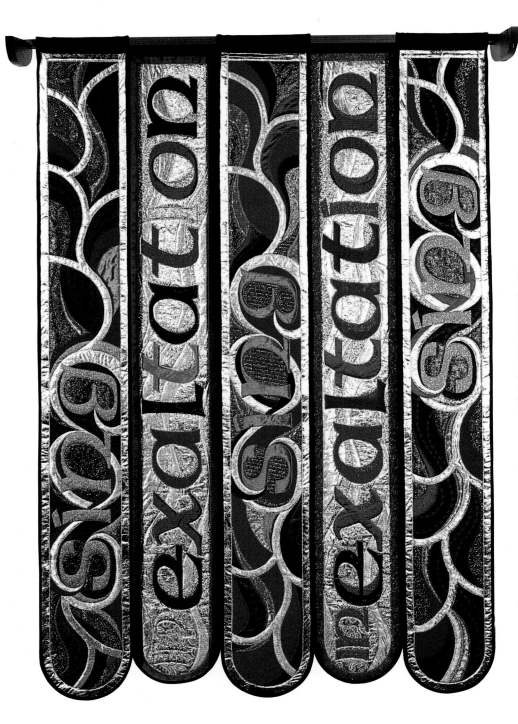

88a, 88b, 88c. *Sing* by Dora Velleman, Armdale, Nova Scotia, Canada. 1987. 64″ x 46″ x 10″ (162.5 x 116.8 x 25.4 cm). Metallics, metallic knits, velvets, nylon net. Machine-appliqué and quilting. Although this gorgeous laudatory piece, like an illuminated medieval manuscript, was not made for a specific church, it has hung for the past two holiday seasons in Dora Velleman's own church (The Universalist Unitarian Church of Halifax) and also in Grace-Church-on-the-Hill in Toronto. It is a fascinating work in that it is multi-layered. A specially designed crossbar allows three separate sections to hang one behind the other thus creating a wonderful sense of movement and depth. "I wanted very much to suggest the changing beauty of stained glass, and I felt that the three-dimensional effect of hanging the pieces at different depths might prompt that response as people walked past," Dora explains. On the back crossbar hang the two pennants worked in the exquisite metallic fabrics that Dora likes to use, bearing the word "Exaltation." On the next bar, some three inches (7.6 cm) in front, hang three similar pennants, but worked this time with the word "Sing." A fine net fall appliquéd with pretty angels with trumpets is then suspended from the front crossbar to provide yet another layer of interest. Unfortunately, no photograph could do proper justice to this intriguing construction, so we were obliged to show the net fall separately (fig. 88b). Not

content with providing a richly textured front for the congregation to admire, Dora felt that officiating clergy should also be given inspiration, so the back of each of the five pennants is appliquéd with the same pattern of angels as those on the net fall, but worked in plain gold fabric (fig. 88c). The back and front of each pennant is made separately and then bound together, and Dora's trademark is evident here. "The technical aspect of my work is very simple," she says. "It is all done by machine. I am somewhat of a fanatic about the sewing machine, for I find it to be an incredible instrument on which to play, and my trademark might be the use of patterned stitching for the quilting lines." You can see this ornamental stitching in figure 85c. (Photographs courtesy Peter Barss)

89. *Burning Bush* by Dora Velleman, Armdale, Nova Scotia, Canada, for St. John's United Church, Halifax. 1990. 96″ x 48″ (244.2 x 122 cm). Metallics, metallic knits, lamé, velvet. Machine-appliqué and quilting. The organist of St. John's Church, Halifax, saw Dora's beautiful work *Sing* (see fig. 88) at an exhibition and persuaded his church to commission a hanging from her for their chapel wall. The piece was designed to hang behind an altar table, but at the dedication service Dora discovered that the committee liked it so much that they had moved the table to one side! She now feels that without the table "it looks a little top-heavy." The construction is the same as *Sing*: a richly textured background overlaid with a net fall. The theme for this inspiring piece is taken from Exodus (chapters 3 and 4:1-17), where God appears to Moses in the flames of a burning bush and tells him of his destiny. Dora has used the Greek letters Alpha and Omega to represent God (see Revelations 1:8) and a descending dove as the Holy Spirit. The brilliant colors of the spiraling flames echo the coloring of the stained glass in the church. Dora says that when she works, she often starts out in one direction but ends up in quite another. "I don't know why this happens, but it may be that when one element does not work as well as it should, I try something else that leads to something else—and something else. I'm sure that I am not alone in this experience!" (She is not, but it is comforting to know that a supremely talented artist like Dora also muddles through like so many of us!) (Photograph courtesy Leo Velleman)

90a, 90b. *Celebrating the Covenant* and *Living Water* designed by Polly Lees, Lindsay, Ontario, Canada, and made by members of the Sunday School for the Cambridge Street United Church, Lindsay. Five years ago, Polly Lees was asked to undertake some sort of a project with a senior Sunday School class at her local church. "We had no banners at the time and, although I had never made a quilt, I like looking at them, so we decided to give it a whirl!" Polly writes. "We made three in three years; *Celebrating the Covenant* (fig. 90a) was our second one, and *Living Water* (fig. 90b), the third. The children enjoyed choosing fabrics and sharing ideas on symbolism, and I found it a useful way to get young teenagers to discuss deeper values." Both banners have traveled. *Celebrating the Covenant* was used at a church conference in Lindsay in 1986 and was then taken to another conference in Oshawa in 1991 at the organizer's request. *Living Water* began life as a logo for the church, but when the planning committee of the Bay of Quinte Conference at Brocknille chose "Living Water" as their theme, the children suggested they should make a banner for the conference. "We had very little time; some of the original group had moved on, so we had new children to teach, but we made it, and the banner was on stage during the four-day event." Nowadays, these beautifully made banners hang opposite each other in the sanctuary of Cambridge Street Church. The names of the youngsters who worked on them are: Judene Bailey, Jeff Broderick, Melanie Clark, Amanda Crocker, Kirsten Davis, Julia deKoker, Kristen Graham, Rebecca Graham, Matt Holloway, Aaron Hughes, Lesley Jackson, Karyn Lackey, Kim Parish, Sean Peters, David Plewes, Jeff Snoddan, Nancy Sweetnam, Steve Sweetnam, Adam Walden, and Clarence Yu. (Photographs courtesy Ken Grace)

90a. *Celebrating the Covenant*, 1986. 49″ (124.4 cm) in diameter. Cottons, hand-appliqué, and quilting. The inspiration for the design comes from Hebrews 8:8-10. "Now this is the Covenant that I will make with the people in the days to come..." The white candle symbolizes Jesus as the Light of the World, and the dancing flames represent the Holy Spirit. The rainbow is a symbol of God's covenant with Noah (Genesis 9:12-13), and the three figures walking along represent God's family journeying home toward God's eternal love. Polly made the piece circular "because the circle, having no beginning and no end, indicates eternity."

90b. *Living Water*, 1988. 37″ (94 cm) in diameter. Cottons, beads, hand-appliqué, and quilting. The biblical reference for this lovely piece is John 4:14: "The water I shall give shall be a well of water springing up into everlasting life." The three streams of water flowing out of the vessel represent the gift of loving, caring, and sharing, while the vessel itself represents all of us through which the Living Water flows.

91. *Children's Banner* made by Shelagh Aiken, Ottawa, Ontario, Canada, for the Church of St. Thomas the Apostle, Ottawa. 1987. 46½″ x 31½″ (118 x 80 cm). Cottons, cotton blends, gold braid, cords. Hand-appliqué, embroidery, and quilting. In 1987, the Church of St. Thomas the Apostle held its sixtieth anniversary, and to celebrate the event, Shelagh Aiken made this banner for the Sunday School. "I tried to illustrate stories of Jesus that the children would remember," Shelagh explains. "And as I cannot draw, I took parts of some of the pictures from *The Good News* coloring book. Reading from top left, the panels are: The Epiphany; Fishermen ('I will make you fishers of men'); Jesus with the children ('Let the children come'); the Resurrection in the garden; Jesus and the Apostle Thomas ('doubting Thomas') and at bottom right, you can see our church with the Rector and the church family ('Go forth and proclaim the Good News.')" Shelagh embroidered religious symbols at the intersections of the sashing, and the crest at the top is that of St. Thomas the Apostle. The lively coloring and the imaginative treatment of the figures make this an enviable gift for a Sunday School. (Photograph courtesy the artist)

110

92. *200 Years—The Anglican Church in Canada* made by Barbara Paterson Robson, Halifax, Nova Scotia, Canada, for the Cathedral Church of All Saints, Halifax. 1987. 48″ x 36″ (122 x 91 cm). Cottons. Machine-pieced, hand-appliqué, embroidery, and quilting. This colorful banner was a commission from the cathedral to commemorate the 200th anniversary of the Anglican Church in Canada. The celebrations were held in Halifax, because this is where the Canadian Anglican church was actually founded. The center motif, based on a bishop's miter, cleverly incorporates the ship as a symbol of the church and at the bottom a stylized fish, the ancient emblem of Christianity. It was the official logo for the celebrations. The embroidered names in the background are those of churches in the city of Halifax. Barbara also made a banner for the seventy-fifth anniversary of the founding of the cathedral. She is a member of the group, the Piecemakers, who are now working on a commission—a set of quilted banners—for another church in Halifax. (Photograph courtesy the artist)

111

93. *All Things Bright and Beautiful* made by Betty MacGregor, Mississauga, Ontario, Canada, for the First United Church, Mississauga. 1989. 84″ x 45″ (213.3 x 114.3 cm). Silk. Strip-piecing, hand- and machine-appliqué. Betty MacGregor is a noted textile artist and was commissioned by friends of the late Susan Rowland to make a memorial hanging for the church that Susan attended during her lifetime. The inspiration for this artistic piece was taken from the hymns sung at Susan's memorial service: "All Things Bright and Beautiful," "For the Beauty of the Earth," and "The Lord of the Dance." Other images include the fish, a symbol of the early Christian church; a donkey representing peace; "The Lord of the Dance"; a butterfly for the Resurrection, and a dove as the symbol of the Holy Spirit. Note the clever appliquéd lettering around the border. Betty has undertaken commissions for other churches in Canada, and some of her work is included in the Massey Foundation Permanent Collection and the Museum of Civilization, Ottawa. (Photograph courtesy Gwen MacGregor, Toronto)

94. *God Who Touches Earth with Beauty* designed and made by Mary Jane Moreau, Toronto, Canada, for the Liturgical Arts Festival in Toronto. 1989. The banner was later hung in HighPark/Alhambra United Church where the artist's husband was the minister. 116″ x 31″ (295 x 80 cm). Cottons, silks. Hand- and machine-piecing, hand-quilting. Here we have another unusually striking hanging inspired by a hymn, this time one of the artist's favorites. She tells us that she wanted to express the value of an integrated approach to life. "By using a building-block pattern in the quilt, I hope to convey the idea that the various elements of our lives should fit together; each building up, one upon another, to create a solid construction." The base of the hanging represents the earth. On it rests a church with an illuminated pathway indicating that God is the true foundation. Above that nature is symbolized in the green and red areas, while the purple ovals represent mankind and also the grape as a sacrament of communion. Near the top, blue arcs represent water—the source of life and of baptism, and finally, the yellow area shows the Holy Spirit in the form of a descending dove with the Star of Bethlehem, Jesus Christ himself, in the center. Mary-Jane's recent marriage to a United Church minister and her return to Ontario from a northern Alberta mining town marked a turning point in her career as a full-time quilt artist. In Alberta, she worked in isolation. "I was quite unaware that unlike many people, at least quilts were going to church!" she says. Now her liturgical work provides a bridge between her career and that of her husband, which excites them both. (Photograph courtesy the artist)

A Pilgrim's Guide
to Australia and New Zealand

Australia and New Zealand, when they were discovered by Westerners in the late 1700s, seemed marvelous new worlds filled with strange and wonderful plants and creatures. Captain Cook arrived in Botany Bay in 1770, and felt that he had come upon a kind of earthly paradise, but after the British Government had digested the news of these discoveries, it was fallen man they decided to send there.

The British were faced with a problem that we know today—severe overcrowding of the prisons. Hitherto, convicts sentenced to transportation had been sold to contractors who shipped them out to the southern colonies in America and sold them as cheap labor to plantation owners. The American War of Independence had put a stop to this convenient system, so the discovery of Australia and Tasmania (known in those days as Van Dieman's Land) provided a heaven-sent solution. In the future, the convicts would be shipped to the far end of the world.

In 1788, Arthur Phillip, the designated governor of the new settlement, set sail with ten vessels and a thousand souls, including, as a hurried afterthought, the Reverend Richard Johnson, to act as chaplain. The convicts ranged from petty thieves and ruffians, frauds and forgers, to murderers and, no doubt, a quota of innocents. They came from the underworld and from working- or middle-class backgrounds and men, of course far outnumbered women. The first penal colony was established at Sydney cove in 1788, and the transportation of convicts to Australia continued until 1868. In all, some 160,000 convicts were transported and two-thirds of these arrived between 1820 and 1850.[23]

Jesus said, "I have not come to call the righteous but sinners," so the Reverend Richard Johnson set to work accordingly. He was an Evangelical Christian, and he set the stamp upon the Australian church for its first years. He was followed by an even more energetic man, the Reverend Samuel Marsden. These pioneers were responsible for the classical architecture of the early churches of which St. Matthew's Church, Windsor, New South Wales, built in 1822, is a perfect example (fig. 95).

In the first two colonies, New South Wales and Van Dieman's Land, Marsden visited all the penal settlements and early settler stations, tirelessly taking the Gospel to convicts and the first generation of the free born. He also journeyed to New Zealand to take the Gospel to the "Noble Savage," the Maori people. He set the church in New Zealand upon its initial course as a missionary church to the Maori people.

Meanwhile, in Australia, society diversified and proliferated. Irish convicts, who had been transported with their priests, brought Roman Catholicism to the territory. Free settlers came—Presbyterians, Methodists, Congregationalists—bringing the whole gamut of denominations from the British Isles and Ireland to the new country.

Patchwork was soon to follow. Elizabeth Fry (1780–1845), the English Quaker who had done so much to improve the conditions of women prisoners and their children in Newgate, realized that something needed to be done to alleviate the intolerable conditions of the women destined for transportation to the new colonies. She persuaded the authorities to introduce changes that would make the journey more bearable, and with the help of a committee called The British Society of Ladies, provided each woman prisoner with a bag of "useful things" for the journey. From 1818 up until the start of her final illness in 1843, Elizabeth Fry visited a total of 106 ships and took 12,000 convicts under her wing.

The contents of the bags were chosen with care, for in addition to copies of the Bible, items of clothing, cutlery and simple toiletries, the women were also given the necessary sewing equipment to make a patchwork quilt, including "2 lbs of patchwork pieces" donated by Quaker drapery merchants in Manchester (fig. 96).

The idea was that making quilts would occupy the women during the long voyage and provide evidence of needlework skills on arrival in Australia, but they might also yield a bonus. En route, the ships called at Rio de Janeiro, where a quilt could be sold for a guinea, and there was also always the possibility of a sale in Sydney.

For many years, it was thought that none of these convict quilts had survived. Apart from wear and tear, the quilts would have had little sentimental value to their makers and as Margaret Rolfe points out in her book, *Patchwork Quilts in Australia*, "Ex-convict women may not have wished to hand on to their children any reminders of their former unhappy past."

Then in 1987 a miracle occurred: a convict quilt was discovered in Scotland. It had been made during the voyage of the *Rajah* that set sail for Van Dieman's Land from Woolwich on April 5, 1841 and arrived in Hobart some three months later (fig. 97a). The surgeon's journal of the voyage records that the prisoners "appear to be of much better character than usual," and certainly care seems to have been lavished in the making of the quilt. There is considerable variation in the stitching, which confirms that several women must have worked on it, but the inscription on the back is very neatly done (fig. 97b).

Just how this quilt found its way back to Scotland is a mystery. The family that owned it had no connection with the Quakers, but it has been suggested that it was sent back to England with the idea of presenting it to Elizabeth Fry to show that her philanthropic work had not been in vain, but there is no evidence to support this theory. The quilt was acquired by the Australian National Gallery in Canberra in 1989.

Whether or not these convict skills were put to use in

95. Francis Greenway was a famous convict architect who built a number of churches in the new colony, but the construction of St. Matthew's, Windsor, a masterpiece in the English Renaissance style, caused endless problems. A young builder called Henry Kitchen bid for the work and construction began in 1817. Kitchen was one of the few men besides Francis Greenway in Australia at that time who had any architectural experience, but even so there were quarrels, and rumors of poor materials and bad workmanship abounded. In the end the governor was forced to intervene. The church was consecrated by the Reverend Samuel Marsden in 1822, and it promptly became the center of Windsor's social life. The bands of the local regiments stationed in the town marched through the streets each Sunday to the church, which caused great delight to the residents, and they also played the music for the hymns. In 1864 and 1867, after appalling floods in the area, St. Matthew's became a refuge for the local farmers and their families. This charming watercolor by an unknown artist shows the church in the early days before the surrounding land was built over. Windsor Church, 1834. Watercolor, 9″ x 11″ (22.7 x 28.8 cm). (Rex Nan Kivell Collection NK 2178; National Library of Australia)

The embroidered panel text reads:

1818-43 **ELIZABETH FRY** visited every ship taking women convicts·children to Botany Bay

106 ships, 12,000 souls

Women used to be taken to the docks in irons in open carts·This was ended·many people helped to improve shipboard conditions

School·sewing groups were started for those who wished

Each woman was given a bag of useful things

96. The Quaker Tapestry from which this illustration is taken is a crewel embroidery of seventy-seven separate panels that celebrates the work and spiritual insights of the Religious Society of Friends (known as the Quakers) since it was founded by George Fox in 1652. The inspiration for the tapestry came from a small English boy named Jonathan, who in 1981 wanted to learn more about the Quakers, and knowing that his Sunday School teacher, Anne Wynn-Wilson, was a gifted embroiderer, said, "Why not tell the story in embroidery rather than drawings?" Anne Wynn-Wilson took as her model the eleventh-century Bayeux tapestry in France, and designed her tapestry so that anybody who wanted to could join in the project. Eventually, more than 2,000 people in eight countries were involved in the making of it! This particular panel is one of two celebrating the work of Elizabeth Fry, who did so much to alleviate the plight of women prisoners transported to Australia in the nineteenth century. She won the right for the women to travel without fetters, she organized work for them to do on the ships, and arranged for help when they arrived in the new colonies. Each woman was given a "bag of useful things," which included the necessary equipment to make a patchwork quilt. As you can see from this panel, which was embroidered by children in Australia and England, the bag included one ounce of pins, 100 needles, nine balls of thread in different colors, one pair of scissors, one thimble, one pair of spectacles, and two pounds of patchwork pieces! (Photograph courtesy The Quaker Tapestry Scheme)

97a. For many years it was thought that none of the convict quilts had survived; then in 1987, this quilt turned up in Scotland. How, or why it was sent to Scotland from Australia remains a mystery, but the inscription shows that it was made on board the convict ship *Rajah*, which left for Van Dieman's Land (Tasmania) on April 5, 1841. Among the 180 female convicts were two tailoresses, several dressmakers, and a Miss Kezia Hayter from the Millbank Penitentiary, who had been recommended to the wife of the governor of the new colony by Elizabeth Fry. It is thought that she probably supervised the making of the quilt. There also appears to have been a "gentlewoman" on board, and it was almost certainly she who worked the finely stitched inscription in figure 97b. The convicts' pack of "patchwork pieces" usually consisted of dress-weight fabrics, but the central panel on the quilt is made of chintz, and considerable skill has been expended in cutting and piecing this prized fabric. It is suggested that this so-called "gentlewoman" may have donated the chintz to the prisoners, and perhaps this is why the quilt was considered too good to be used and why it was sent "home." The chintz still has its original glaze, so the quilt has probably never been washed. The quilt was acquired by the Australian National Gallery in 1989. (Photograph courtesy the National Gallery of Australia, Canberra)

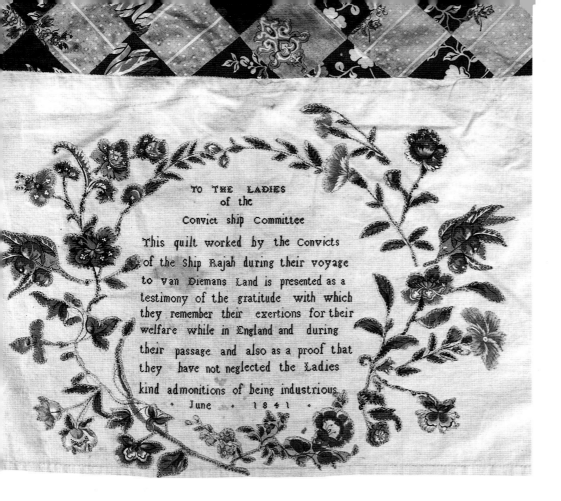

TO THE LADIES
of the
Convict ship Committee
This quilt worked by the Convicts
of the Ship Rajah during their voyage
to Van Diemans Land is presented as a
testimony of the gratitude with which
they remember their exertions for their
welfare while in England and during
their passage and also as a proof that
they have not neglected the Ladies
kind admonitions of being industrious
· June · 1841 ·

97b. The inscription on the back of the *Rajah* quilt has been worked in silk, and the stitching is similar to the best embroidered samplers of the period, which suggests that it was not the work of a female convict, but that of an unknown "gentlewoman" who was probably one of the passengers on the ship. The pattern for the actual lettering may have been done by another passenger, the Reverend Rowland Davies, who was returning to Van Dieman's Land to build a new church at Longford. (Photograph courtesy the National Gallery of Australia, Canberra)

98. This Sunday School banner was made in 1815, probably by the daughters of a family of Protestant missionaries called Hassell, who came to Sydney as refugees from Tahiti on board *The Duff* in 1798. The eldest son, Thomas (1794–1868), started a Sunday School in their home at Parramatta in 1813, when he was just a teenager. The parents were weavers by trade, and being moderately literate, together with other families in their group, did active work in setting up schools in the area. Parramatta Sunday School banner, 1815. Silk thread on silk. 28″ x 25″ (72 x 64 cm), including fringe. (National Library of Australia)

99a, 99b. The arrival of Spanish Merino sheep in the early 1800s transformed Australia, which is now the largest wool producer in the world. This is a modern cope, and it was made in soft Merino wool by Mayanne Boom-Clarke and her mother, Mildred Clarke, and was presented to the sixth Bishop of Canberra and Goulburn, K.J. Clements (fig. 99b), on the occasion of Mayanne's marriage in 1963. The beautifully painted design on the satin orphreys is based on the native passionflower, which is found in Queensland and New South Wales. The leaves are large and ornamental, and the flowers are orange-yellow with bright orange stamens. The tiny brilliants that Mayanne and her mother stitched on the tips of the stamens, and the stones that you can see on the clasp of the cope and on the bishop's miter, came from a costume worn by a famous Australian operetta star called Gladys Moncrieff, popularly known as "Our Glad." The costume manager of the opera saved them when a lot of old costumes were being burned—yet another example of the way the church is not above borrowing from the laity for its vestments! The cope is now owned by the bishop's daughter, Mrs. Diana Body. (Photographs courtesy Mrs. Body and Heide Smith, Canberra)

making vestments for the early churches is not known because no Australian-made vestments from this early period have been identified. A Sunday School banner dated 1815 has been found, and the simple stitching suggests that it was not done by a professional hand (fig. 98). Undoubtedly, altar frontals and banners were used, and indeed, advertisements in the *Church of England Messenger* suggest that the Victorian Ladies Work Association and guilds of various city churches were prepared to undertake church work.[24]

The larger churches and cathedrals imported vestments from Europe just as American churches did, and some of these are still in existence. In the Roman Catholic church, where chasubles were worn as much as three times a day, it was apparently the custom to burn vestments when they wore out, although it is unclear why such drastic action had to be taken.

The arrival of Spanish Merino sheep in the early 1800s spurred the development of farming and the opening up of new colonies, initially in south Australia. Merino wool was used for the twentieth-century vestments seen in figures 99a and 99b.

The discovery of gold in 1851 brought new immigrants and further widened the economy. Cultivation of sugar opened new areas in Queensland, and the development of a rust-resistant wheat and the technique of refrigerating meat enabled Australia to become an important supplier of European markets. Local industries grew. Australia began to take on the robust earthy character we know today.

Meanwhile, the Aborigines fared badly, debauched by a Western society unable to comprehend the values of a Stone Age culture—a tragedy with some parallels with the history of the American Indians in the United States. The Aborigines had no concept of needlework until it was introduced by Western missionaries, but a rare patchwork quilt made about 1848 by Aboriginal children, possibly on a mission station, exists in the National Library of Australia, Canberra.

In New Zealand things developed differently. When Bishop George Selwyn arrived in the Bay of Islands he commented: "The lot is fallen unto me in a fair ground; yea, I have a goodly heritage." But he found himself the pastor of a divided flock. Missionaries and Maoris on the one hand; settlers on the other. Out of these tensions came the unhappy incidents of the Maori wars, which marred the early history of the country.

European communities started from whaling stations and appear to have moved through three stages. The first was the "Eucalyptus period," when big sheep stations were the center of life and worship, and were visited by itinerant clergy. Typically, eucalyptus trees ringed the station in the open countryside. Then came the "Pine period," when the big stations were broken up into individual farms, with a clump of *Pinus Insignis* by the homestead, and the center of the community was the school. The "Cypress period" came next, with houses clustered in a village around a church, and the gardens were separated by cypress hedges. Toward the end of the last century this was the pattern of rural society in New Zealand.

By the early twentieth century, a rich bourgeois society had evolved in Australia. In 1901 the Australian states combined to form a Commonwealth. Australian cultural consciousness developed into the precocious talents of a young nation full of abilities in literature, drama, art, cinema, and television out of all proportion to the size of its population. New Zealand, quieter, more rural and isolated than Australia, also evolved its own cultural personality, again with a wealth of talent disproportionate to its small population.

As the twentieth century advanced, Australia and New Zealand learned the hard way (like Americans before them!) that loyalty to the "Old Country" was a one-way street. The Australian and New Zealand forces (AN-ZACS) felt sacrificed in the Dardanelles in World War I and in Crete and Tobruk in World War II, while their home countries faced Japan undefended. Since World War II, with Europe turning itself into a Common Market, Australia and New Zealand have found themselves abandoned by their traditional trade partners. They have been spectacularly successful in finding new markets for their produce in the Pacific area, notably Japan. Australians and New Zealanders are now everywhere in business, including Singapore, Hong Kong, and Tokyo. The new orientation has brought new outlooks.

In the different Australian and New Zealand cultures there are some common features. They are fascinating countries with special geographic, scenic, and climatic phenomena and with a unique plant and animal life. It is from these differences that liturgical artists draw their inspiration. In the illustrations that follow you will see the wealth of cultural talent that seems to flourish in these southern climes.

ANDREW LIDDELL

100a, 100b, 100c. *Lent and Advent Set* designed and made by Ruth Hingston, Watson, Australian Capital Territories, for the church of St. John the Baptist, Canberra. 1988. Altar frontal: 43½″ x 106½″ (110 x 270 cm). Lectern Fall: 23½″ x 15¾″ (60 x 40 cm). Polyesters, rayon, polyester satin. Machine-appliqué. We begin our pilgrimage in the Southern Hemisphere with a gloriously colorful set of church furnishings that use typical Australian imagery to convey theological meaning. Ruth Hingston, who is a professional illustrator, textile designer, and teacher of fashion design, explains that she continues to be curious "how best to express our spirituality as white people who have come to live in a land like Australia," so she decided to use a familiar scene for this particular work. "The gum tree is a well-known image in the Australian landscape, and individual trees have a special meaning for the aboriginal people. They sit in the shade of gum trees during the heat of the day waiting for the coolness of the evening. Lent and Advent are both times of waiting, of preparing, for death and resurrection at Easter and for birth at Christmas." She decorated the chasuble and lectern fall (figs. 100b. 100c) with leaves "because leaves are the parts of the tree that move in the wind, just as people are moved by the wind of the Holy Spirit." Fascinated by the effects of color, Ruth used intense hues because she wanted to communicate the depth of passion that Christ experienced in the Garden of Gethsemane. She originally intended to silkscreen-print her design, but then switched to appliqué because she felt that texture and richness of color could be more effectively achieved with fabric. She deliberately chose to work with synthetic fabrics because they retain their vibrancy of color for much longer than natural fibers and are less vulnerable to insect damage, a common hazard in Australia. The chasuble is worn here by the Reverend Andrew Knight. Ruth received financial assistance when making these wonderfully scenic vestments through a special projects grant from The Visual Arts and Crafts Board of the Australian Council. (Photographs courtesy Michael Pugh)

101. *Cope and Miter* designed and made by Ruth Hingston, Watson, Australian Capital Territories, for the Archbishop of Adelaide, the Very Reverend Ian George, for his consecration as bishop. 1989. Wool/polyester crepe, silks, silk velvet. Machine-appliqué and quilting. For this commission, Ruth says that she did a considerable amount of research into the role of a bishop. "I was interested in the images, symbols, and colors that signify such a role within the church and community. I also looked at other figures of rank and selected a period of literary history that interested Ian [the Archbishop]. Black, gold, and white seemed to be a special combination of colors associated with rank." The splendid design on the hood draws upon the Old Testament story of Elijah annointing David. "It seemed to me that people are annointed by God, and by the people, to a particular position of service, so the gold rivulets represent the oil being poured on the head of the person being annointed." (This same design of rivulets continues down the orphreys on the front of the garment and across the morse, that is to say the clasp.) The gold triangles around the edge of the hood symbolize the Trinity. Ruth's involvement with ecclesiastical work began when her husband was appointed curate to the church of St. John the Baptist in Canberra where the rector, a great patron of the arts, was Ian George, then Archdeacon. "He saw the making of vestments as part of a spiritual process, "Ruth says, "and looking back on it now, I see that he was right." (Photograph courtesy Michael Pugh)

102a, 102b, 102c. *Communion Table Cloth and Lectern Fall* by Margaret Roberts for the Weston Creek Uniting Church, Canberra, Australia. 1984. Communion cloth: 46″ x 120″ (117 x 304 cm). Lectern fall: 55″ x 14″ (140 x 36 cm). Cotton, polyester, brocade, vinyl. Machine-piecing and appliqué. Margaret Roberts wanted to make a gift to the chapel when the new parish center was opened in 1984, so she designed this richly colored cloth to allow the congregation to share in the celebration of God's goodness and His promises to His people. Because the communion table is sometimes used for a service in the round, the cloth covers both the front and the back of the communion table, and Margaret worked it in one piece ("it took over our large dining-room table for weeks!"). She wanted to use symbols that were important to her, so she chose "the Cross, a symbol of salvation and redemption, for the front panel, and I tried to convey the idea of the power of the Cross radiating out across the hills, plains, and sky of our earth (fig. 102a). Across the top of the table is a rainbow (fig. 102b), a symbol of God's promise that never again will He cover the earth with a flood. On the back panel, I placed the dove of peace (fig. 102c). The machine-embroidered river on the lectern fall (fig. 102a) represents the stream of living water that God has promised to those who desire it." Notice how the pieced construction of Margaret's work is echoed in the stained-glass "patchwork cross" by Annette Manton. (Photographs courtesy Robert Patterson)

103. *Banner for the Church of Our Savior* made by Barbara (Hohnberg) Watson, Katoomba, New South Wales, Australia. 1986. 83½″ x 39½″ (212 x 100 cm). Recycled synthetic fabrics, some cotton. Strip-piecing, reverse-appliqué, hand-appliqué, embroidery, machine-quilting. For years the Lutheran Church of our Saviour in Springwood had no permanent home. Services were held in a school hall, and the congregation made do with the surroundings until one Sunday the pastor suggested some banners might add visual atmosphere to their worship. Although Barbara was a busy woman (her family owned a dry-cleaning business, and she did the repairs and alterations in the shop), she says that the words "banners for the church sent me reeling with excitement." She made various banners over the next few years, learning the truth of the words "the Lord will provide." ("Inspiration and fabrics came in unexpected ways, and time was always given to me.") In 1986, the church was about to move to a permanent home, so she embarked on the stunning hanging you see here. Inspiration came from the cover of an American vestment catalogue showing a wall mosaic in an unnamed church. Barbara redesigned the central figure and superimposed it over a view of the Australian Blue Mountains and a famous local rock formation called the "Three Sisters" at bottom left. She explains that "the sweeping bands of color represent the whole of God's creation, with Our Lord as the one unchanging rock. The flames of the Holy Spirit and the Alpha and Omega symbols remind us that He is Savior for all time." The fabrics were recycled from second-hand evening wear (sold in the church "Opportunity Shop"), but Barbara could not find anything suitable for Jesus's robe. "Then one day, a young woman brought a ruby-red satin evening dress into our shop for alterations. The bits left over were exactly what I needed!" (Photograph courtesy Michael Small & Associates, Katoomba)

104a, 104b. *Advent Banners* made by Barbara (Hohnberg) Watson, Katoomba, New South Wales, Australia, for St. Mark's Lutheran Church, Epping, New South Wales. 1989. 102″ x 36″ (259 x 91.6 cm). Silk, viscose, cotton, cotton blend. Machine-pieced and quilted. When Barbara was commissioned to make some advent banners for St. Mark's Church, she thought of patchwork because it tied in with the angular lines of the chancel window, but she badly needed some design inspiration. "As usual," she says, "it came in an unexpected way! One brittle, frosty morning in early spring I walked over to my son's house to deliver an urgent phone message. There were plane trees along the street that were just starting to break out their new leaves, and as I squinted up to marvel at the wonder of new life, the rising sun was right behind the branches. The frosted buds glittered and reflected the sunlight into interlocking rainbow circles. There was my Advent banner pattern, a tribute to new life!" The basic interlocking-circle pattern was adapted from one that Barbara had seen in *Quilter's Newsletter Magazine*, and she placed Advent symbols in the central spaces. One banner has the four candles for the four weeks of Advent (fig. 104a), while the other contains the symbols of the long-awaited King; the lamp trimmed and ready; the manger; the crown, and the Chi Rho, the sacred monogram of Christ the King (fig. 104b). These attractive banners are a testament to Barbara's considerable talent. (Photographs courtesy Wally Gilbert, Berowra)

105. *Triptych* designed by Robyn Body, Kaleen, Australian Capital Territories, and made by members of the congregation for St. Simon's Anglican Church, Kaleen. 1988–1989. Panels 1 and 3: 39″ x 39″ (100 x 100 cm); panel 2: 39″ x 79″ (100 x 200 cm). Wool, cotton, polyester, corduroy, sheepskin. Machine-piecing and quilting, hand-appliqué and embroidery. Australian artists like to incorporate native scenery and symbolism in their work, and this enchanting triptych is no exception. It was made for the sanctuary area of a hall that is being used temporarily by St. Simon's for services during a major three-stage building program. "The expanse of wall was so big that we didn't feel able to make one piece to cover the whole area, so the idea of a triptych was born," the designer, Robyn Body, explains. "Each panel illustrates one event in Christ's earthly ministry—His Baptism in panel 1, the Crucifixion in panel 2, and His Ascension in panel 3—but the typical Australian background continues in each panel so as to make one complete picture. Also the sky changes from early morning to late evening in the three panels. St. Simon's parishioners are from the suburbs of Kaleen and Giralang, which are both aboriginal words from the Wiradjuri tribe—'Kaleen' means water and 'Giralang' means star, so both these symbols appear. The royal bluebell (*Wahlenbergia Gloriosa*), the symbol of the Australian Capital Territories, is also included in each panel. The people in the panels represent the disciples, or us (some people have identified themselves as the sheep wandering aimlessly around the paddock!), and the road disappearing into the distance signifies Jesus's command to us to proclaim the gospel throughout the world." The names of the other ladies who worked on the triptych are: Judith Arentz, Doreen Tuckwell, Janice Dengate, Sandra Gill, Edith Clatworthy, Deanne Reynolds, Ellen Davies, and Phillipa Pratten. (Photographs courtesy Heide Smith, Canberra)

106. *Regeneration* designed by Marlene Greenwood, MacGregor, Australian Capital Territories, assisted by Gillian Hunt, Margaret Reeson, and fifty-eight members of the congregation for Uniting Church Kippax, Holt. 1987. 275″ x 118″ (700 x 300 cm). Polyester, hand-painted silk, satins, brocades, velvets, silver lurex, and other fabrics. Hand-piecing, appliqué, embroidery. Machine- and hand-quilting, beading, tatting, and trapunto. From 1978 until 1987, Uniting Church services were conducted in a primary school, where pieced and embroidered banners helped to disguise gym equipment and other school paraphernalia. When the new Parish Centre at Kippax was being planned, Marlene Greenwood had a vision of a major wall hanging to be an integral part of the church architecture just as a stained-glass window might be. Some themes were discussed at a meeting in 1985, which included the centrality of the Cross and a desire to express the message in terms of nature and Australia. Up until this point, Marlene had deliberately kept her mind clear of any detailed ideas about the project, except the dimensions (which were huge) and the Cross. As a busy person, she expected to find it difficult to allocate enough uninterruped time to finish the design, but she saw God's hand in what happened next. She became ill and was ordered to lie prone in bed with eyes closed for two weeks. In the enforced silence and isolation, Marlene focused on the Cross, and when she was well enough to begin her initial drafts, much of the design was already complete in her mind! As the work got underway, the only fabrics that needed to be purchased were those for the background, the silver cross, and the interfacing. The rest were donated by the congregation and in almost every case pieces were found that exactly matched Marlene's original cartoon. She feels that the design was "given" to her. We do not have enough space to list all the symbolism in this marvelous hanging, but the basic theme is Christ as the Light of the World. The hanging was consecrated on July 17, 1987, with special music composed by Adrian Greenwood, aged twelve years. (Photograph courtesy Justin Dumpleton and Martin Sonderen)

107a, 107b. *The Communion and the Trinity* designed and made by Lucy Hill, Caloundra, Queensland, Australia, for the Chapel of The Glebe. 1989. Each hanging is 32″ x 48″ (81 x 122 cm). Cottons. Machine-piecing, hand-appliqué, and quilting. Lucy Hill is a professional quilt-maker, and she was asked to make these two lovely, tranquil wall hangings for a chapel at The Glebe, a hostel for the frail aged that had recently opened in her home town of Caloundra. "The chapel is nondenominational and very modern with soft gray carpets and furnishings, so I chose the coloring of the hangings to complement them. My commission was to represent Holy Communion and the Trinity. In *The Communion* (fig. 107a) I used the well-known symbols of grapes and wheat, but the quilted lines radiating from the chalice suggest the flow of blessings. Because a circle is eternal, I used it in *The Trinity* (fig. 107b) to represent the Father. The cross symbolizes Jesus and the white dove is the Holy Spirit." The hangings were installed in time for the official opening of the hostel in July 1989, and they must give great pleasure to the many people seeking comfort and solace in the chapel. (Photographs courtesy Chris Pemberton)

108. *The Risen Christ* made by Ria Wilson, Bonbeach, Victoria, Australia, from a drawing by Meg Heriot for St. Joseph's Church, Chelsea, Victoria. 1987. 137½″ x 47″ (350 x 120 cm). Cotton, taffeta with organza overlay, laminated furnishing fabric. Machine-appliqué and embroidery. Hand-beading, reverse-appliqué. When Meg Heriot's drawing, *The Risen Christ*, was displayed at St. Joseph's Catholic Church, Ria Wilson thought the figure was so joyful and alive that she felt inspired to make it into this marvelously dramatic three-dimensional banner. "All the time I was working on it, I felt that God was working closely with me and I thanked Him as I worked," Ria says. "The banner is only used at Easter to celebrate the risen Christ, and it is unrolled ceremoniously and hung up while the choir sings the 'Gloria.' It has been a joy and inspiration to many people in the congregation." Ria has made a number of other hangings for the church, but she feels that this banner is her best work. (Photographs courtesy the artist)

109. *The Dossal Hanging* designed and made by Beverley Shore Bennett, Waikanae Beach, New Zealand, for St. Paul's Cathedral, Wellington. 1990. 29′ x 15′ (8.85m x 4.58m). Furnishing fabrics (discontinued samples), cottons, linens, manmade fabrics. Machine-piecing and appliqué. Beverley is a professional artist whose main interests are stained-glass design and embroidery, and her work is to be found in many cathedrals, churches, and chapels in New Zealand. This wonderful hanging is enormous, and Beverley says that she would really have preferred to make a glass mosaic to fill the space it now occupies, "but it was too costly, so the next best thing was to try and create the same effect with fabric. I have always deliberately avoided using the term 'patchwork' because I associate it with 'bed covers,' and I was worried that the dossal might become known as 'the biggest patchwork quilt in New Zealand'! What I did not anticipate was the power that the medium has to attract the viewer. I have designed hundreds of successful stained-glass windows over the years, but none has drawn so much favorable comment as this hanging. Patchwork is a wonderful way of creating tone and color effects for ecclesiastical work." When planning her design, Beverley took into account that St. Paul's Cathedral was in the heart of the city, and many people can be found during the day sitting and meditating in the cathedral. It seemed important, therefore, to create something that would not be intrusive or too strident. As the cathedral is also used for concerts, she felt it was equally important to make a statement as to whose house it is. "As time passes, I am becoming more and more aware of God's influence—of the way He has shaped my life to His purpose." More of Beverley's beautiful work can be found in her book, *A Key to Embroidery*. (Photograph courtesy the artist)

Spiritual Inspirations

Spiritual Inspirations

"And she had thrice been to Jerusalem,
Seen many strange rivers and passed over them,
She'd been to Rome and also to Boulogne,
St. James of Compostella and Cologne."[25]

The Wife of Bath

Like the Wife of Bath in Geoffrey Chaucer's *Canterbury Tales* (see fig. 110), our pilgrimage has taken us to many places and revealed marvelous liturgical work embellishing cathedrals and churches in different countries around the world. It has been uplifting to discover so much, yet there must be more that has been missed or has not come to light on this journey. This could lead to more discoveries by other pilgrims.

A pilgrimage never ends, because when the pilgrim arrives at the destination the experience leads on to spiritual voyaging and perhaps, ultimately, to spiritual inspiration. The mind takes over where the feet leave off. This book is the result of a personal pilgrimage that began on the site of the tomb of St. John the Apostle near Ephesus in present-day Turkey. As Andrew and I stood there, I suddenly saw in my mind's eye the Ephesus of the early Christian refugees, the presence in the city of St. John, who is believed to have fled to Ephesus with Mary the mother of Jesus, after the expulsion of the Christians from Jerusalem in A.D. 37.

The house where Mary is alleged to have lived still exists outside Ephesus and is a place of pilgrimage for Christian and Muslim alike, for St. Mary has the distinction of being the only woman to be mentioned in the Koran. She is mentioned four times, and she is honored by Muslims as the mother of the "prophet" Jesus.

As we mention in the introductory essay, the financial market in Ephesus became the church of St. Mary the Virgin. In those days, canon law only allowed a church to be dedicated to saints who had lived, or died, in the area. My spiritual voyaging then led to St. Paul and the riots that he caused in the theater in Ephesus (Acts 19:23-41), and the quest for more information about these early Christians grew.

It was from this moment that a book began to take shape, and because I write books about quilts, it turned into this book about the religious spirit in quilting. It was a subject I knew nothing about at the time, but when I was led to start a group to make new vestments and banners for our church in London (see figs. 40a, 40b, 41, 42a, 42b, 43a, 43b, 43c, 43d, 44a, and 44b), it became apparent that we had joined a religious patchwork movement that was worldwide.

The quilts in this section are the result of similar spiritual voyaging, inspiration, quest, and guidance. These particular works do not hang in churches but are exercises in faith for personal or seasonal use, for contemplation and for prayer. In creating them, quilters have found personal spiritual enrichment. In looking at them, readers will find themselves moved to their own visions. As you will find in this fabric art, quilting, stitching, and embroidery have been and will always continue to be acts of spiritual devotion in themselves.

JILL LIDDELL

135

110. *The Marriage of Chaucer at St. Mary de Castro, Leicester* designed and made by Linda Straw, Leicester, England. 1992. 33″ x 27″ (83 x 68 cm). Silks. Machine-appliqué, quilting, and embroidery. As we end our pilgrimage around the world, it is perhaps fitting that we should start the inspirational section of the book at the wedding of the great English poet, Geoffrey Chaucer (1340–1400), whose narrative poem *The Canterbury Tales*, one of the chief glories of English literature, captured the jollity of a motley crowd of medieval pilgrims making their way to the shrine of St. Thomas à Becket at Canterbury. Linda is a noted British quilt artist who specializes in pictorial hangings on historical subjects and this superb piece was commissioned by the East Midlands Region of the Quilter's Guild of Great Britain for the Guild's Heritage Collection. She chose Chaucer as a theme because he is one of her heroes (she made a fine quilt based on *The Canterbury Tales* in 1985, which was sold to an American buyer) and because she discovered by chance that he had connections with the region. "When I was told by the verger of St. Mary de Castro in Leicester that Chaucer had married Philippa de Roet there in 1367, I nearly knelt down and kissed the floor!" Philippa de Roet was the sister-in-law of Chaucer's lord and mentor, the great John of Gaunt, Duke of Lancaster and Earl of Leicester. Although Chaucer might not recognize the church now because it was reconstructed in the nineteenth century, the triple arcade that you can see on the right side of Linda's quilt survives from his time as do the pictorial floor tiles. The guests would be familiar, however, for each of them appears in *The Canterbury Tales*. On the bride's right stands the Merchant, behind him you can see the Nun and the Nun's Priest, and seated in the pew at the back is the Wife of Bath whose conjugal reminiscences are among the most entertaining parts of the poem. In the foreground struts the cockerel, Chanticleer, one of the characters in the fable recounted with such mastery by the Nun's Priest. (Photograph courtesy the artist)

111. *Spring Song for Nicholas* by Josephine Ratcliff, Preston, Lancashire, England. 1991. 54″ x 36″ (137.4 x 91.6 cm). Shaded taffeta, cotton furnishing and dress fabrics, lawn. Hand- and machine-appliqué, reverse-appliqué, machine-quilting, hand-embroidery. In this final part of our pilgrimage, which is devoted to quilts with a spiritual theme, some are exercises in personal faith, some have been inspired by church architecture, and some by favorite hymns, such as this charming hanging exalting God's creation. Josephine trained as a musician, "so when our grandson, Nicholas, was baptized, it was my privilege to play 'All Things Bright and Beautiful' at the service. Calligraphy is one of my husband's hobbies, so he designed and drew the verse from the hymn for me just before we set off for a long holiday in the United States, part of it spent in the company of young Nicholas and his parents. I scooped up a handful of blue, green, and mauve embroidery silks and was grateful to have something absorbing to embroider during the long waits we had at the airports. Six months later, I spotted two rolls of shaded taffeta in blues and greens in the sales that were just waiting to be used in this project!" Nicholas is delighted with his enchanting quilt and takes great pleasure in pointing out the birds, animals, bugs, and flowers to visitors. "My church and my faith are central to my life," Josephine explains, and she has undertaken many ecclesiastical commissions (one of her beautiful pieces can be seen in figure 49. (Photograph courtesy Christopher Ratcliff)

112. *Nuit de Noel* by Monique Clarac, Royat, France, from a drawing by Constant. 71″ x 63″ (180 x 160 cm). Machine- and hand-appliqué; hand-quilting. This superbly joyful nativity scene is used by Monique Clarac to broadcast the Christmas message at her home each year. The inspiration came from a drawing, signed with the name "Constant," that appeared on the cover of a children's magazine called *Fripounet*, published in 1979. Monique altered the disposition of the figures and completely changed the coloring. She says that she discovered patchwork in 1985 and was "immediately seduced!" After fifteen years of sculpture (wood, stone, and clay), quiltmaking arrived at an opportune time for her. "Now that I had reached the age of sixty-three I could no longer lift my sculptures, so I have devoted myself to patchwork ever since." Several of Monique's other quilts have been hung in major national as well as local exhibitions in France. (Photograph courtesy Jean-Jacques Petiard, Images Production, Riom, France)

113. *Façade* by Diana Brockway, Newport, Gwent, Wales. 1991. 58″ x 36″ (148 x 91 cm). Cottons, cotton blends, lamé, Indian silk and sari fabric, Indian madras cotton. Machine-pieced and quilted, hand-stitched beading. Church architecture has inspired fine pieces by several quilters of which this dramatic work is one. (The artist has achieved an amazing three-dimensional effect with her Log Cabin construction, but having seen it, I can vouch for the fact that the quilt is indeed flat!) Diana was struck by three strong visual images in Florence Cathedral after visiting and photographing it while on holiday. One was the strong blue and gray coloring, the second were the bays on the façade, and the third was the arcading on the apse. Diana drew the outline of the design full size on graph paper, but only the top row of arches as these would be repeated six times. She says, "I did not foresee the Escher-like illusion that occurred in the center panel whereby the top lines of arches appear like a bay while the bottom ones look like an alcove, but I regard this as a happy accident." Diana is attracted by the decorative possibilities of architecture, especially churches, because of her art background. She taught art and architecture in schools and at a college of art in England. (Photograph courtesy the artist)

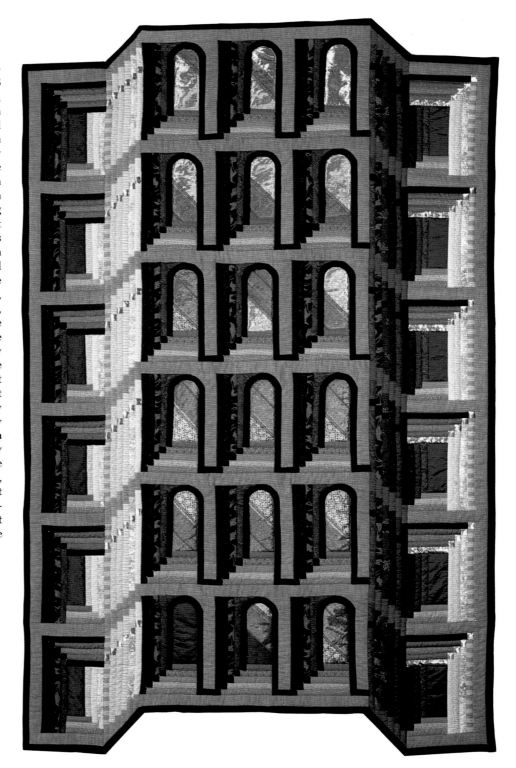

114. *Basilica San Marco* by Sandra Townsend Donabed, Wellesley Hills, Massachusetts, United States. 1990. 60″ x 60″ (153 x 153 cm). Cottons, cotton blends, hand-marbleized and hand-painted fabrics. Machine and hand-piecing, hand-appliqué, and quilting. Here are two more striking pieces inspired by church architecture. In the spring of 1989, Sandra visited Italy and was struck by the interiors of the great cathedrals that "... speak of the hands, centuries ago, that built these magnificent creations to glorify their God." This quilt was inspired by the floor in the famous Basilica of San Marco in Venice, and the quilt in figure 115 was inspired by the series of domes in the cathedral of Siena. In this piece, Sandra has used reverse-appliqué to imitate the aged marble that had been chipped and worn away with time, and she hand-marbleized and hand-painted many of the fabrics. "I became engrossed by the thought of Italian artisans changing the pattern and color according to the materials that were available." She says that she was "transfixed" by the similarities of these ancient floors to traditional patchwork patterns, but it is suspected that church tiles were probably the inspiration for many of those early American designs. (Photograph courtesy David Caras)

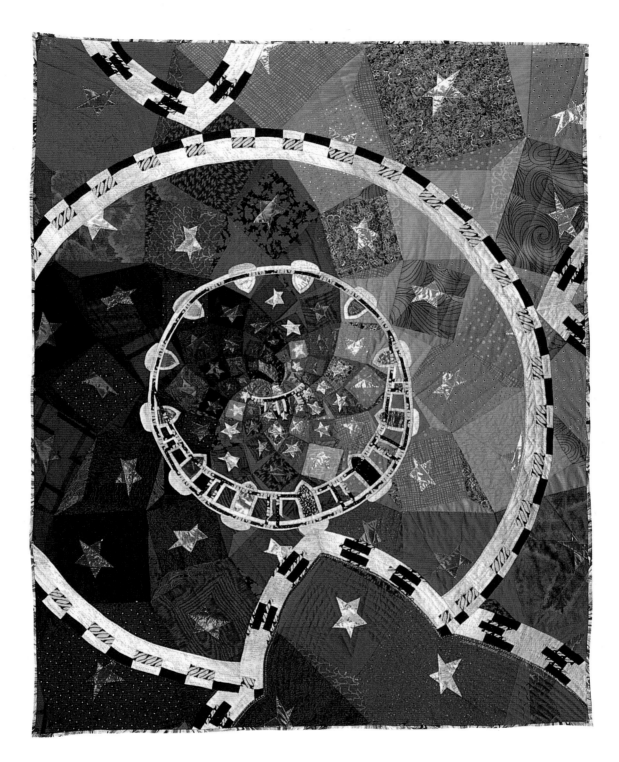

115. *Duomo di Siena*. 1990. 65″ x 50″ (165.3 x 127 cm). Cottons, metallics, cotton blends. Machine-pieced, hand-appliqué, and quilting. Sandra was fascinated by the interior of the dome of the Cathedral of Siena and the way that the light played upon the blue and golden stars. "The architect built it in such a way as to lead the viewer up to heaven." Notice the walkway and windows that she has created at the top of the dome and the effect of light entering on the blue ceiling. (Photograph courtesy David Caras)

116. *Basilica Armen-Odzun* by Deborah Melton Anderson, Columbus, Ohio, United States. 1989. 42″ x 39½″ (106.8 x 100.5 cm). Cottons. Machine-appliqué and quilting. This staggering architectural piece by Deborah Anderson was inspired by the remains of an Armenian basilica of the sixth or seventh century. The artist had been studying a black-and-white photograph of the basilica, when the terrible earthquake of December 1988 occurred. She dedicated this quilt to the victims. "The ruins are gray and weathered, yet they still 'speak' of a holy place, a house of worship and prayer. The Byzantine-influenced Armenian architecture with its multiwindowed dome seems to draw an individual to a new state of mind. I have given the basilica new life through color—the burning votive candles and the red carnations (themselves a symbol of life) recall the wounds of Christ and the wounds of the victims of the earthquake." Deborah is noted for her liturgical work (see her altar frontal in fig. 63), but she confesses that once in a while she needs to work intuitively and not on commissioned work that has to be approved. This marvelous quilt is one of her "intuitive" pieces; another is shown in figure 117. (Photograph courtesy Kevin Fitzsimons)

117. *Calvary Cross and Crown Transformed* by Deborah Melton Anderson, Columbus, Ohio, United States. 1982. 44″ x 44″ (112 x 112 cm). Cottons. Machine-appliqué. "The Crown of Thorns is a powerful image," says Deborah Anderson, the maker of this fine contemplative piece, "and I suppose I was influenced by the many triangles that occur in piecework (although I used machine-appliqué to make this particular quilt) to help me make the connection with thorns. I think of Lent as a deeply emotional and introspective time, and I use this as a personal banner during Lent." She explains that the design is meant to be read from the outer edges toward the center and that by doing this, the title becomes clear. "The heavy gray-purple cross is transformed into a thinner gold cross of victory. The dark thorns of the outer crown are transformed into the gold ornamentation on the inner cross." For nearly thirty years Deborah has been inspired by the silk-screened patterns of Marimekko fabrics from Finland. She first came across them when she was a student in Cambridge, Massachusetts, and they were sold in a store just around the corner from where she lived. She used these fabrics in this quilt and in the architectural piece in figure 116. (Photograph courtesy Kevin Fitzsimons)

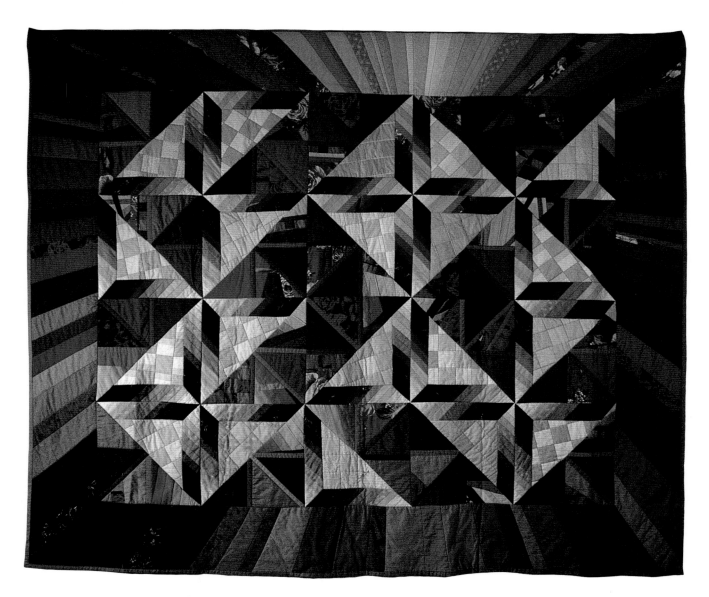

118. *Amazing Grace* by Pamela Thibodeau Hardiman, St. Louis, Missouri, United States. 1987. 62″ x 78″ (157.7 x 198.4 cm). Cottons. Machine-pieced, and quilted. Pamela says that she did not set out to make a quilt with a Christian theme, in fact it was the other way around. This inspirational design led her to a deeper Christianity. "My husband and I had been trying for about a year to have a child (after many years of waiting for me to finish graduate school), and it was becoming clear that something was radically wrong. In the midst of this, I took a workshop with Nancy Crow that literally changed my life. The task she set us was well defined: design a simple block suitable for strip-pieced fabric. I took off from that moment, and I found a window where a door had closed." Pamela was led to liturgical work and says that her faith has grown with her art. You can see some of her marvelous commissioned pieces in figures 61a, 61b, and 61c. And the story has a happy ending, for Gregory Joseph was born three years after *Amazing Grace* was finished, and her quilt also inspired another liturgical artist. Sister Josephine Niemann, S.S.N.D., saw a photograph of *Amazing Grace* in *American Quilter Magazine* and says that she recognized the Cross as a "wonderful symbol of the glorified Christ" and borrowed part of it for a banner she made for the Seattle cemeteries (see fig. 66d). She subsequently met Pamela and the two of them became close friends. (Photograph courtesy the artist)

119. *Consider the Lilies* by Joanne Kost, Sandy Hook, Connecticut, United States. 1984. 53″ x 24″ (134 x 61 cm). Cottons, cotton-blends. Machine-piecing, hand-appliqué, and quilting. In addition to her commissioned work (see fig. 72) Joanne has made a series of quilts with biblical themes. "Although we are a Christian family, I did not consciously set out to make biblical quilts," the artist says. "I am a person who has always found inspiration in words, and the Bible 'spoke' to me. I feel that I was divinely led." After she had completed her biblical series, Joanne started on another series called "Nature's Windows" that simulate stained glass. She continued to use biblical texts for inspiration. *Consider the Lilies* (from Matthew 6:28) was the first one in this new series. Joanne has given up quiltmaking for the time being. She is now a self-employed folk artist and makes primitive dolls and an original line of canvas figures. This illustration was published in *Quilter's Newsletter Magazine* #172. (Photograph courtesy Bob Kost)

120. *Reina del Chielo* by Margaret Hays, Mill Creek, Washington, United States. 1988. 52″ x 35″ (132.3 x 89 cm). Silk, satin, lace, taffeta, cardboard Christmas cards, buttons, net, beads. Hand-piecing, appliqué, embroidery, and quilting. Mexican folk-art Madonnas, with their immense, ornate halos and strong, primary colors were the inspiration for this marvelously rich hanging. Margaret says she is attracted to monumental mother figures, and this was the first of three Mexican pieces. Her ingenuity is evident in the materials she uses. "I made the outer ring of the halo from Christmas cards of Madonnas that I had collected over the years. I cut each one in a circle, covered it with net, then framed it with silk-covered cord and sewed it in place." Figure 121 illustrates an example from another of Margaret's "Mother and Child" series, and a third tactile soft-sculpture hanging of hers appears in figure 73. (Photograph courtesy Richard E. Hays)

121. *Icon #8*, 21″ x 14″ (53.4 x 35.6 cm). Velvet, taffeta, polyester blends, silk, cording. Hand-appliqué and quilting. "I was so inspired by the glorious icons that I saw on a trip to the (then) Soviet Union that I have made twenty-five fabric icons, each one unique," Margaret says. "I suspect that they are Mother Earth images as well as icons. The mother and child image is one of the oldest religious images, going back into prehistory before the time of Christ. Even the prehistoric mother fertility figures have the child implied, even if it is not visually present. It is one of my favorites." This lovely piece is the eighth in the series, and it accurately captures the coloring and religious tranquility of a genuine Russian icon. Like most of Margaret's work it was bought by a private collector. (Photograph courtesy Richard E. Hays)

122. *The Good Shepherd* by Paula Hawkinson Hottovy, Dwight, Nebraska, United States. 1990. 93″ x 70″ (236.6 x 178 cm). Cottons. Hand-pieced and quilted. The idea for this superb mosaic quilt emerged in Paula's mind. "I truly believe that God spoke to me and asked me to do this quilt for Him," she explains. "I decided I would use a cross-stitch pattern and began searching everywhere for one that would be applicable. One day in the mail I received an unsolicited booklet advertising cross-stitch kits, but only one was on a religious theme. It was called "The Good Shepherd," but when I ordered it, the pattern contained only Christ and the sheep, so I drew my own background using graph paper." Not even knowing if her technique would work, Paula cut half-inch (1.2 cm) squares and began piecing them together, a few squares at a time. "It was as if God were with me, because as I finished each step it would come to me how to do the next one." The quilt contains 21,625 squares, and Paula quilted around each square so that the quilt does have the tactile appearance of a genuine mosaic. It was hung in the American International Quilt Association's exhibition at Houston, Texas, in 1991, where it attracted considerable attention. Paula is making a second quilt and says she will "just go along with my quilting and see if I am 'inspired' to do more." We hope that she will be for this is an outstanding piece of work. (Photograph courtesy the artist)

123. *Amish Sweetgrass* by Win Burry, Toronto, Canada. 1985. 43½″ x 43½″ (110.6 x 110.6 cm). Cottons. Hand-piecing, appliqué, and quilting. We end our pilgrimage in Canada with an unusual and colorful piece that uses Native Canadian symbolism to express spiritual values. Although two similar pieces by Win were included in the Liturgical Arts Festival held in Toronto in 1989, she does not consider herself to be a liturgical artist. "They are spiritual pieces," she says. "Since I began my research into our native Indian art some years ago, I discovered that their shamanism combined with my father's Quaker heritage has become a foundation of 'truth' for me. This particular quilt is based on the art style of Norval Morrisseau, the 'father' of the Anishnabec school of Native Artists. The central figure of the thunderbird is the protector of native people. Within him is the shaman and within the shaman is the white circle that is the 'The Light of Christ Within.' The four circles represent the four seasons of the year and the four ages of man. They are bisected to indicate the duality of all things and the communicating lines show that everything is interdependent and goes on forever." Win pieced the border in the Crown of Thorns pattern "because Christ lived and died in order to show us the reality of our nature in relationship to God." She made the quilt for her husband, C. James Burry, and the title comes from its Amish coloring and from the way the Indians burn sweetgrass as a form of incense in their ceremony of purification. (Photograph courtesy Don Stanfield)

Ways and Means

Many ingenious techniques have been used to make the vestments, banners, and quilts that you have seen in the color plates and it would be impossible to give details of them all. Altar furnishings and vestments have changed their shape many times over the centuries in response to changes in the liturgy, and they will no doubt do so again. Today, vestments and forms of decoration vary according to the theological position of the parish, so there is no "correct" pattern as such. Altar frontals can be rigid constructions stretched over a frame to prevent wrinkling, or soft throwover cloths. They can be wide or narrow, rectangular, or cruciform in shape.

In churches where vestments are used, the Gothic style of chasuble is commonly worn, for which a pattern is given in section 10 below, but there is no fixed rule about this. The shape can vary according to the taste of the artist and the priest for whom it is made. For example, the Danish artist Mana Torne revived an ancient form of tabard for the two chasubles shown in figures 28a and 28b. "Ministers are just as varied in shape as everybody else," she says, "so I thought it would be a good idea to make my chasubles symbolic and not obviously like a cloak." The tabard shape was also ideally suited to her geometric designs.

Banners and hangings come in many different forms, and you will find a selection of the more popular shapes in section 6 below, but the dimensions must be determined by the place in which they are to hang.

Therefore, the purpose of this part of the book is to give you some guidelines, and some ways and means of construction that are based on the experiences of the artists whose work is illustrated in the book. I have not included directions on how to do patchwork and appliqué because there are many good books available that deal specifically with these subjects.

In the section called CHRISTIAN SIGNS AND SYMBOLS, you will find some of the more popular Christian signs and symbols, together with some original patterns taken from work included in the color plates, which the artists have been kind enough to allow me to include.

1. DESIGN

Design is always a stumbling block, and even professionals find it difficult to work up a satisfactory design, but as a major patron of the arts the church has always been pragmatic, admitting new styles in every period and encouraging the natural talents of the people.

a) *Themes*
Traditional symbolism is important, but so is the art of our own age and one's own region. When you are searching for inspiration, do not be afraid to use what you know. We have seen how Canadian and Australian liturgical artists like Nancy-Lou Patterson and Ruth Hingston (figs. 86 and 100a, 100b, 100c) drew on local ethnic sources to produce wonderfully spiritual pieces, and how Louise Leonard adapted native Alaskan dance masks for her banner in figure 79a.

Explore what interests you. The British designer Jane Lemon was interested in the plight of the inner city, so she designed a striking contemporary altar frontal showing a skyline of highrise buildings for one of Britain's oldest Gothic cathedrals (fig. 35). Contrasting the old with the new as she has done can be visually stunning.

If you are interested in the environment, then you might consider a botanical theme. Look at the marvelous scenic pieces exalting the natural world by Susan K. Turbak and Joanne Kost in figures 69a, 69b, 69c, and 72. Colleen Hintz chose God's creation for her vestments in figures 68a, 68b, 68c, 68d, and put a hibernating chipmunk on the stole because it was her daughter's "favorite image!"

b) *Church Architecture and Decoration*
Take your camera into the church and photograph the interior for ideas. Obvious sources are tile patterns or carvings. The effective "cathedral window" border that Gerry Enger used on her Advent hanging in figure 77b was inspired by some carvings she found on the pulpit, but Linda Fowler found inspiration for her marvelous hangings (figs. 70a and 70b) in architectural features such as stairways and arches. You may be surprised by what hidden beauty your camera will reveal.

c) *Use your Bible*
A favorite text can be a useful source of inspiration. It can provide you with a theme, or you can incorporate the actual text in a design (see diag. 3). Most dictionaries of quotations include the better-known and therefore more-illustrative texts. Hymns can also spark ideas.

d) *Use a photocopier* to enlarge motifs and patterns from books. The law permits you to make photocopies for your own personal use, but you may not make copies of a

pattern for distribution to your friends, or to your students, without prior permission from the publisher. Greeting cards provide a good source of ideas, and the artists are usually delighted to know that their design will live on in the form of a banner, so try to get their permission.

e) Advertise for an artist

If you have ideas but cannot draw, advertise in the church magazine for someone to help you. Many people can draw well but do not want the responsibility of designing a banner from scratch. Persuade your artist to make you a full-scale drawing, as you can use this for templates and as a pattern to cut out background fabric, interlining, etc.

f) Composition

Designing for the church is like designing for the stage. Your work will be viewed from a distance and needs to combine bold color and drama in order to convey its message, but also provide some close-up interest. Donna Garofalo (fig. 71) says that she always includes details that are not immediately noticeable so that the congregation can enjoy making "little discoveries."

Generally speaking, a design is more interesting if the main focus is not placed dead center. Obviously, there are exceptions, for some altar frontals demand a central motif, but a well-known trick is to divide the surface area of your design into thirds vertically and horizontally. You can either place your focal points where the dividing lines cross (diag. 1), or use these divisions as a guide (diags. 2 and 3).

You can also base your design on an oval, a triangle, or an S-shape, or you can base it on a diagonal. But do not forget the importance of space, which acts as a "rest area"

Diag. 2

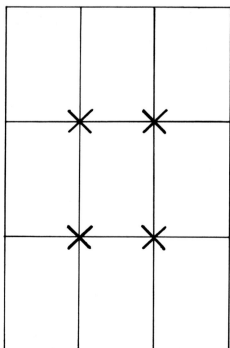

Diag. 1

Diag. 3

for the eye. Every area of activity needs to be offset by an area of tranquillity.

g) *Thinking time*

Finally, do not underestimate the importance of "thinking time." Creativity needs time to evolve. Discuss your ideas with friends, or with your group, but then let the resulting thoughts simmer in your mind for a week or so. You are designing for God's house, so it is vital that your design does not send out the wrong signals.

2. COMMISSIONS

When you have been given a commission, make sure that everybody understands the brief before you start work. Priests are busy people, and some find it difficult to articulate exactly what it is they want, so it is advisable to present a properly thought-out design, preferably in color, for the minister to show the church council exactly what it is that you have in mind.

When Jane Lemon undertakes a commission, she photographs the setting in the church and blows the photograph up on a color copier. Then she draws an appropriately scaled mock-up of her design in color and glues it in the correct position on the photocopy. "People find it difficult to visualize," she says. "This way they can see exactly how my finished design will look in the church." Diagram 4 shows a mock-up that Gill Bryan did for a laudian altar cloth for her church in London. (See section 9 for an explanation of how to make a laudian cloth.)

Diag. 4

a) *Beware of camels*

Because so much of church work is done by committees, your design will probably have to be vetted by a number of people, all of whom will have something to say about it, but resist the temptation to try and please everybody. Remember the old saying, "a camel is a horse designed by a committee." Do not let your design turn into a camel!

b) *Fees*

This is a thorny problem because money is so often in short supply, but if you are a professional artist, you should always charge a realistic fee for your labor. Here is a formula you may care to try.

1. Cost out all your materials. That is to say all the fabrics including interlining, lining, threads, embroidery floss, etc., and then add 10%.

2. Multiply this figure by three.

3. If the work is likely to be complex and therefore time-consuming, add on a bit extra to cover this.

4. The resulting figure is *your fee*. On top of that you should charge the church for the cost of the fabrics and any expenses such as photocopying, reasonable traveling costs, etc.

Members of the congregation are often glad to pay for fabrics as a memorial to a friend or relative, so in order to defray costs try advertising your needs in the church newssheet. You can credit the donor in a nicely embroidered label on the back of your piece.

3. COLOR

Fortunately, the church provides us with a set of liturgical colors as a basis with which to work. The common sequence in use in Roman Catholic, Anglican, and Protestant churches in Europe, the United States, Australia, and New Zealand is as follows:

Advent:	Blue, violet.
Christmas:	White, or a festive robe clearly distinguishable from the colors for the rest of the year.
Epiphany:	White.
Sundays after Epiphany:	Green.
Ash Wednesday:	Violet.
Lent:	Violet, or no color, such as unbleached linen (sometimes known as the Lenten array).
Good Friday:	Black, violet, red, or no color.
Pentecost:	Red.
Trinity Sunday:	White.
Trinity to Advent:	Green.
Saints' Days:	Red.

The easiest way to find suitable color schemes to go with these liturgical colors is to buy a good color-wheel from an art shop. There is a science to color, and a wheel will give you the various color combinations that will work well together.

An illustration of how useful such a color-wheel can be occurred when we were making the altar frontal in diagram 5 (see also fig. 40). We wanted to copy the colors in the stained-glass window behind the altar, so we chose a blue-green for the background and yellow-orange and red-orange for the cross.

Diag. 5

The window also contained a rather strong blue, but when we cut out the fish in this color, they looked quite wrong. A quick glance at the color-wheel showed us that in a standard four-color harmony combining blue-green, red-orange, and yellow-orange, the fourth shade should be blue-violet. When we used blue-violet for the fish, the altar frontal came to life.

Some color-wheels are so arranged that you can "dial" a harmony, and it will give you all the tints, tones, and shades of the various colors as well.

- A *tint* is a color that has been diluted with white and is what we would therefore call a pastel.
- A *tone* is a color to which gray has been added, which mutes the color; in other words it is a medium tone.
- A *shade* is a hue to which black has been added to create a dark color.

Diagram 6 gives you the basic color-wheel that consists of the three primary colors: yellow, blue, and red; the three secondary colors, which combine two primary

colors mixed in equal amounts: green, orange, and violet; and the six tertiary colors, which are mixtures of primary and secondary colors: yellow-green, blue-green, red-orange, etc.

From this color-wheel you can work out six standard harmonies (see diagrams 7–11), but you should avoid using colors of equal value, equal intensity, or in equal amounts. Variety is essential, so always try to incorporate a selection of the appropriate tints, tones, and shades in any color scheme.

1. *Monochromatic*. This is a harmony made up of the tints, tones, and shades of *one* color combined with black, white, gray, or neutral tones such as beige, etc. (this harmony is not illustrated).

2. *Analogous*. This is a harmony that is composed of colors with a "family" resemblance, i.e. three colors that fall within a 90° angle on the color-wheel: yellow, yellow-green, and green (diag. 7). To spice up this scheme you could add a complementary color from the opposite side of the wheel: i.e. red, or red-violet.

3. *Triadic*. For this color harmony, you must combine three colors that are equidistant on the wheel. The classic triadic harmony would be yellow, blue, and red, but a more interesting scheme might be yellow-green, blue-violet, and red-orange (diag. 8).

4. *Complementary*. Every color has a "mate" that is its opposite on the color-wheel, for example, yellow and violet, or yellow-green and red-violet (diag. 9). Complementary colors are perfect accents for any color scheme.

5. *Split-Complementary*. In this scheme you combine one color with the two colors that lie on either side of its complement, i.e. yellow, blue-violet, and red-violet (diag. 10).

6. *Double Split-Complementary*. This is the color scheme that we used for the altar frontal in diagram 5. It consists of two pairs of colors that lie on each side of a pair of complementary colors, e.g. blue-green, blue-violet, yellow-orange, and red-orange (diag. 11).

If you wish to experiment with color schemes yourself, trace diagrams 7 through 11 on clear plastic. Mark the center clearly and lay these circles over the color-wheel in diagram 6 to find the harmony of your choice. (You could also make your own wheel by taking a color copy of diagram 6 and mounting it on cardboard. Most color copiers will reproduce these clear colors very well.)

An important concept to remember is that warm colors advance and cool colors recede. Warm colors are those on the red/orange/yellow side of the color wheel and cool colors lie on the opposite side. Most stone churches need warm colors, and a good tip is to ask the flower-arranging team what colors they find work best.

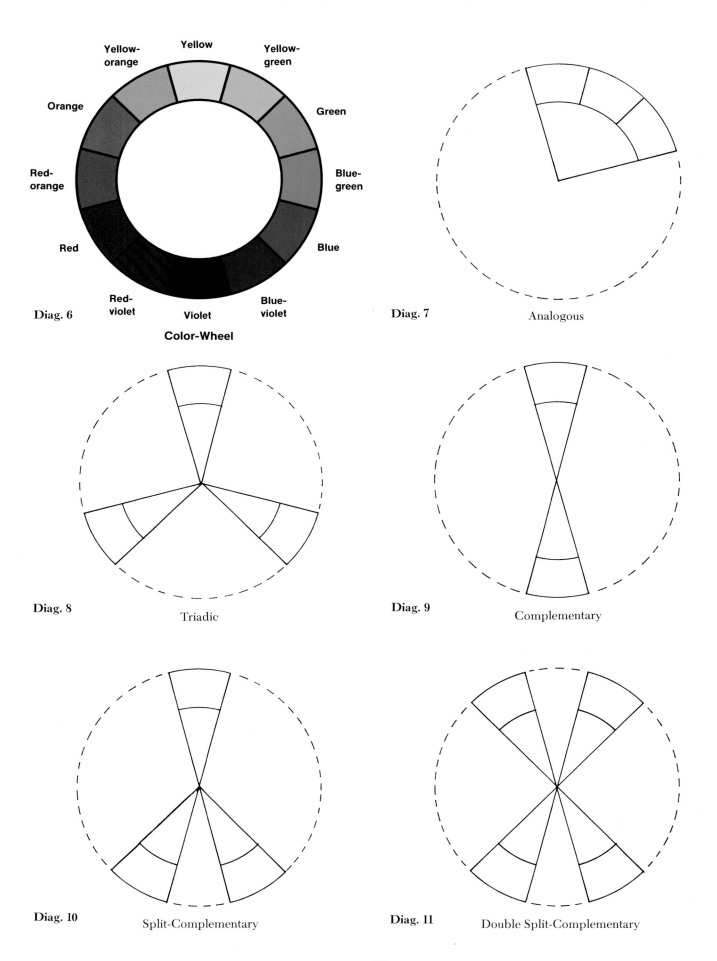

Diag. 6

Yellow

Yellow-orange   Yellow-green

Orange   Green

Red-orange   Blue-green

Red   Blue

Red-violet   Blue-violet

Violet

Color-Wheel

Diag. 7   Analogous

Diag. 8   Triadic

Diag. 9   Complementary

Diag. 10   Split-Complementary

Diag. 11   Double Split-Complementary

You must expect to work with much stronger colors than you would use at home, for you need drama in a church (think of stained glass), and resist the temptation to match everything. The classic method of finding a color scheme is to take a piece of patterned fabric and then "match" a series of colors to it. The result is usually restful, but it is seldom dramatic!

Use a complementary color (one from the opposite side of the wheel) to add spice. Neutral colors such as cream, beige, gray, and tan are also useful because they do not change a color scheme, and muddy colors such as khaki, sludge-green, and olive should not be ignored. These are the colors of nature, and like gray-blue, indigo, rust, and even forest green, will combine with almost any scheme.

There are many books on color theory on the market, but they have their limitations because you will be working with fabric and not paint. Also, you will have to make do with what is available. No department store carries fabrics in the full range of colors. Books on color theory written by quilters are helpful because they deal specifically with fabric, but the final judge of any scheme must be the church itself. *Always* take your fabrics into the church to try them out before you start stitching. Churches are notorious for being badly lit, and even the most scientific color harmony may well die if it has to compete with a dark-gray granite pillar, or the colored reflection from a stained-glass window!

4. FABRICS

Choosing the right kind of fabric can be a problem. Church furnishers usually carry a range of fabrics in the liturgical colors that can be bought by the yard, but these are often traditional fabrics such as damasks, and you may want something more contemporary looking. Furnishing fabrics are the right weight, but you will need to read the labels carefully to make sure that what you are buying is suitable for the conditions in your church.

If your church is heated during the week, it doesn't really matter what kind of fabrics you use, but if it is only heated on Sundays, and has had several hundred years in which to absorb the damp like so many of the churches in Europe, your work will turn into a limp rag in no time if you aren't careful. Here are some of the advantages and disadvantages of the various kinds of fabrics on the market today.

All natural fibers are biodegradable and will be affected by damp and by insect damage. The standard test throughout the world says that cotton and silk will absorb 13% moisture in an atmosphere of 65% relative humidity at an average room temperature of 70 degrees farenheit (20 degrees centigrade). Sixty-five percent relative humidity is equivalent to the atmosphere in an English garden at dusk when the dew is starting to fall, but in some climates you will have to compete with 80-90% humidity (or even higher) in the summer months. Cotton fabrics in these damp conditions can stretch alarmingly.

The colder the church becomes, the less water the atmosphere will hold, and the damper it becomes. When you think of your wash hanging on the line, you will see how fibers swell and stretch when wet, and then shrink again when dry, leaving the fabric wrinkled. Your banner may well behave the same way.

However, not all types of cotton behave identically because the fibers are affected by different dyes and different finishes. In our extremely damp English climate, pure cotton furnishing fabric turned out to be a disaster, but deck-chair canvas, which we used for hangings, stood up very well indeed.

Silk is extremely strong (that is why it was used for parachutes before the discovery of nylon), and because of its beautiful luster it is an ideal fabric for church work. However, silk will fade in strong sunlight (as indeed will most natural fibers) and may grow mold in damp conditions.

Viscose (rayon) is a manmade fiber, which originates from regenerated cellulose, and it is also affected by moisture and does not have much resistance to abrasion, i.e. it will not withstand much rubbing. Its great advantage is that it has very good draping qualities.

If you use natural fibers, you must expect some wrinkling to occur according to the level of humidity. The best way to find out about possible wrinkling is to test your fabrics in the conditions in which they are to be used. Stitch together a quarter yard (20 cm) of your main fabric, interlining, and the backing and hang this up in the church to see what happens to it. Six weeks, preferably during the winter months, is a fair test, and it is worth doing this because you will be spending a great deal of time and energy in making the piece, and a bit of research into the

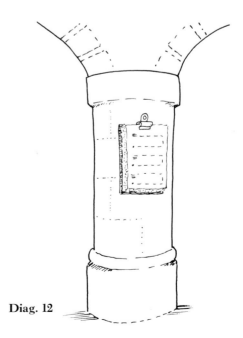

Diag. 12

behavioral qualities of the fabrics will save heartbreak later (diag. 12).

Stretching your work over a wooden frame, or inserting wooden battens across the back of a banner or altar frontal, will help to keep its shape. See section 9 for further information.

Man-made fibers such as terylene, acrylic, dralons, or polyester are more stable than natural fibers, but they will not crease easily and the dyes are often more vivid. They are also resistant to insect damage, but they are difficult to appliqué because they do not take a crease easily.

A mixture is often the best solution. I have found that a fabric containing 55% terylene and 45% wool to be ideal in damp conditions. Linings and interlinings can also cause problems in that they may shrink at a different rate. As a general rule, it is advisable to use the same type of fabric throughout, all natural fibers or all manmade fibers.

5. WORKING METHODS

This section covers adaptations of traditional sewing techniques that various artists have found useful.

a. *Patchwork*

In traditional English patchwork you baste fabric over a paper template of the required shape and then whipstitch the patches together. British designer Beryl Dean evolved a variation of this method that is used today by many British liturgical artists, and which allows a variety of different weights of fabric to be used successfully in one project (see Beryl's pieced cope and altar frontal in figures 33 and 34). Instead of making templates from paper (which have to be removed), Beryl makes them of interfacing and varies the thickness of the interfacing according to the different weights of fabric; thick interfacing for thin fabrics and vice versa. She leaves these templates in the work to give the patches substance and durability. With this type of patchwork, you do not need to quilt, and because the patches have to be individually basted, it is a useful method for group projects.

b. *Appliqué*

The above method also works well for appliqué, for it gives substance to the individual motifs, particularly if you are not planning to quilt the piece. For the lilies on Gill Bryan's banner in figure 42a, cardboard templates were made from the full-scale drawing, and these were used to draw the design on small rectangles of medium-weight interfacing. (Remember to *reverse* your templates so that nonsymmetrical images will be correct on the right side of the fabric.) The interfacing was then pinned to the *wrong* side of similarly sized pieces of fabric, and the outline was then straight-stitched on the machine (diag. 13).

As this banner was a group project, each member was

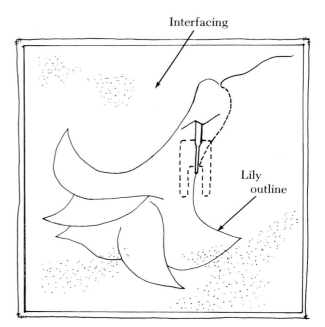

Diag. 13

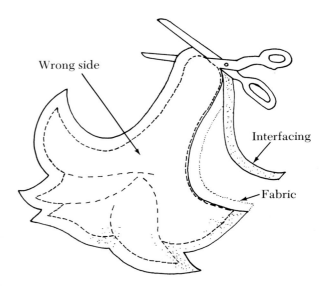

Diag. 14

then able to embroider her lily individually, and after this was completed, we cut the lilies out, leaving a ¼-inch (7 mm) seam allowance, and trimmed the *interfacing* (but not the fabric) back to the machine-stitching (diag. 14). We basted the fabric seam allowance back before stitching the lilies to the background (diag. 15). The stamens were made from flat gold braid that were couched on last. Batting can, of course, be used instead of interfacing if you prefer a softer look.

Working appliqué motifs on separate pieces of fabric (with or without interfacing) is ideal for group projects, because each member can work on different parts of a banner at the same time.

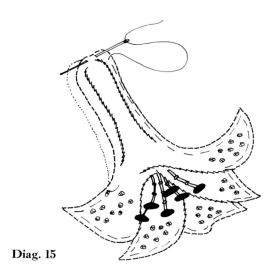

Diag. 15

Diag. 17

c. *Fusible Webbing*

Double-sided fusible interfacing such as Pellon™ Wonder-Under is ideal for fixing motifs or lettering to your background fabric, but unless it is properly applied, it can cause the fabric to wrinkle. A good tip is to lay the interfacing down on an ironing board *sticky side up*, then place a same-size piece of fabric on top of the interfacing *and iron the fabric to the facing* rather than the other way around. That way you can make sure that the fabric is smooth and flat (diag. 16). *Note:* The fabric and the interfacing *must* be the same size in order to prevent glue from getting on the bottom of the iron.

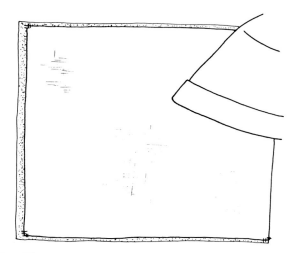

Diag. 16

Turn the fabric over and draw your appliqués on the paper backing, but remember to *reverse your templates*, otherwise the nonsymmetrical images will be the wrong way around (diag. 17). When cutting out the motifs, do not leave a seam allowance and fuse the motifs or letters to your background fabric in the normal way. You can

satin-stitch over the raw edges on the machine, or couch them with wool or cord.

Ordinary fusible interfacing is useful for stabilizing thin fabrics for either piecework or appliqué, but it does not always work well on manmade fibers because you cannot use a hot enough iron to bond it properly to the fabric. It may also alter the look of fabric, for example it can deaden the sheen of some silks. There is a type of fusible cotton on the market, so your quilt shop may have it, and this may work better with silk, but experiment first.

6. BANNER SHAPES

Banners can be any size that is suitable for the church and diagrams 18 a-e give some of the more traditional shapes.

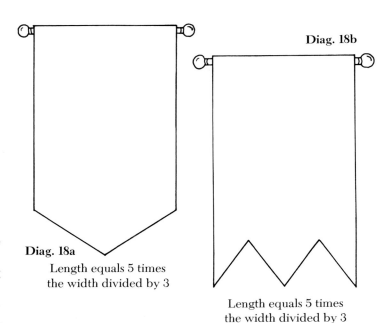

Diag. 18b

Diag. 18a
Length equals 5 times
the width divided by 3

Length equals 5 times
the width divided by 3

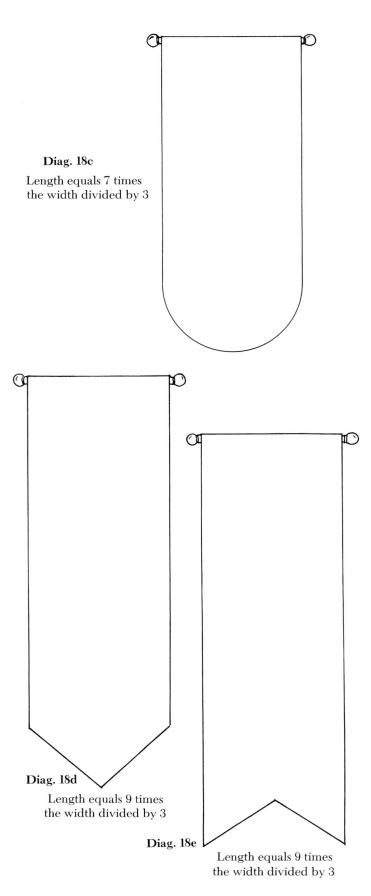

Diag. 18c

Length equals 7 times
the width divided by 3

Diag. 18d

Length equals 9 times
the width divided by 3

Diag. 18e

Length equals 9 times
the width divided by 3

However, determining the correct proportions can be difficult, so here is a useful formula. First, you must decide on an appropriate width, then:

    a. Divide the width of the banner by three.

    b. For a regular banner, multiply this figure by five to give you the length (diags. 18a and 18b).

    c. For a longer banner, multiply by seven (diag. 18c).

    d. For a pillar pennant, multiply by nine (diags. 18d and 18e).

7. MAKING UP THE BANNER

    a. It is advisable to make a full-scale drawing of your design so that you can trace your templates from it, and also use it as a pattern to cut out your background fabric, batting, interlining, etc.

    b. Mark the outline shape of the banner on your background fabric, and cut it out leaving a 1-inch (2.5 cm) seam allowance. Stay-stitch any curves or bias edges.

    c. Trace the outline of the design, using a light box or dressmaker's carbon and apply the motifs.

    d. If you plan to interline, rather than quilt, cut the interlining the *same size* including seam allowances, and with matching thread, lock the interlining to the background fabric at 6- to 8-inch (15 to 30 cm) intervals down the length of the banner to stop it from shifting (diag. 19). Turn over the seam allowance and lightly catch it to the interlining. It is a good idea to lock the lining in one or two places as well.

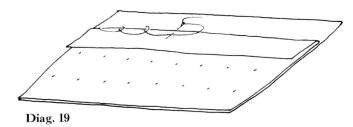

Diag. 19

    e. Stitch hanging strips in place before stitching the lining, or make a sleeve from a strip of folded fabric when the banner is finished.

    f. If the banner is to be used in a processional, decorate the back with some appropriate eye-catching motif or use an interestingly patterned fabric for the lining. The backs of processional banners are visible for a long time as they are carried up the aisle!

8. HANGING THE BANNER

Wooden curtain poles and brackets are an excellent way of hanging banners in the church, but in some denominations (notably the Church of England) wooden brackets may be classified as a permanent fixture for which permission would have to be sought, so check before you start drilling holes in the wall!

Diag. 20

Cheap banner poles can be made from lengths of ¾-inch (2 cm) doweling (or thicker depending upon the size and weight of your banner) with a small wooden knob screwed to each end and darkened with wood-stain (diag. 20). Curtain tie-backs make marvelous cords and tassels for narrow banners. Look at the pillar pennants in figures 43a, 43b, 43c, and 43d to see the effect.

9. ALTAR CLOTHS

As you will have seen in the color plates, altar cloths come in many guises, from formal frontals mounted on stretchers to simple throwover cloths. When a central altar is used and the cloth is to be viewed from several angles, a cruciform shape is ideal. Elizabeth Taylor made her *Renewal* frontal in figure 81 cruciform-shaped, but as the frontal is never taken off the altar, she was able to sew the sides together to about 6 inches (15.2 cm) from the bottom so that the four-sided frontal fitted snugly over the altar (diag. 21). An alternative would be to fasten the sides together with Velcro so that the frontal could be opened out flat for easy storage.

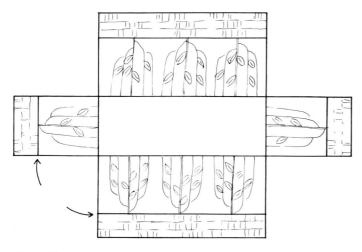

Diag. 21

Eleanor Van de Water simplified the cruciform in her *Glory Frontal* (fig. 65) by working it in two long separate panels that are placed on the altar in the form of a cross. As

the back of the altar was not going to be seen, she only embellished the ends of three of the panels (diag. 22).

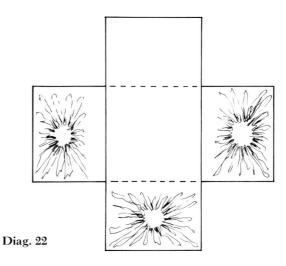

Diag. 22

If you look at Joy Saville's reversible altar cloths in figures 60a, 60b, and 60c, you will see an interesting way of cutting the lower edges of a cruciform-shaped throwover cloth.

For a straightforward suspended frontal that will only be viewed from the front, here is a suitable pattern (diags. 23 and 24).

a. The frontal is made in one long length that stretches from the front, then over the top to approximately halfway down the back of the altar. You will need to measure this area to give you the width and length you need. In most Catholic and many Protestant churches the altar is usually covered with a white linen altar cloth (or cloths) for services, and with a dust cloth at other times. Therefore, the sections of the frontal that run across the top of the altar and down the back will not be seen. Thus, to save money, these unseen sections of the frontal could be made of some type of cheaper fabric such as canvas or heavy cotton (see diag. 23).

Diag. 23

b. Cut out the frontal leaving 1-inch (2.5 cm) seam allowances.

c. The embellished front section should be interlined.

158

Cut your interlining *with* seam allowance and lock it as suggested for banners (see diag. 19). Then lay flat battens across the back and oversew these to the interlining. Turn the seam allowance *over* the battens (making sure that the work is taut) and stitch down (diag. 24). Lock the lining and stitch in place.

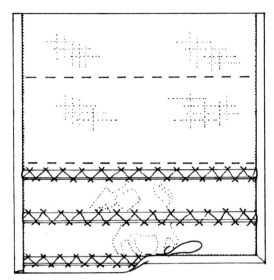

Diag. 24

d. If the embellished section is very heavy, it may be necessary to create a counterweight, in which case make a channel along the back edge of the frontal and insert either a flat wooden batten or a steel rod. If you are making a narrow frontal for a nave altar like the one in diagram 5, where the back edge may be glimpsed from the side, a more decorative rod can be made from a piece of ¾-inch (2 cm) doweling with a wooden knob screwed into each end (see diag. 20).

This type of suspended frontal looks good laid over a laudian cloth, that is to say a throwover cloth that reaches to the floor. This combination is illustrated in figure 41. A laudian cloth is made like a bedspread or a tablecloth, with the corners rounded to create attractive folds (diag. 25). If you plan to seam several widths of fabric together, make sure that the seams do not fall on these folded

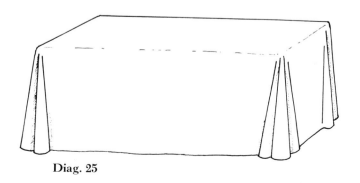

Diag. 25

corners otherwise they will not hang straight. Ideally, such cloths should be lined, but in practice a lining can cause problems because it pulls away from the cloth. If you feel you must line the cloth, then lock the lining to the cloth in the same way as has been suggested for banners.

10. PATTERNS FOR CHASUBLE, STOLE, CHALICE VEIL, AND BURSE

The usual set of Low Mass vestments consists of a chasuble, a chalice veil, and a burse. The chalice veil is used to cover the chalice, and the burse holds the corporal (a small square of fine linen used by the priest during the consecration). During the early part of the service, when the burse is not in use, it stands upright on the altar. The most commonly used form of chasuble is the Gothic style and normally, the chasuble, stole, burse, and veil are made of matching fabric with similar styles of ornamentation. A pattern for a Gothic chasuble is given in diagram 26a, but as has already been mentioned, it is perfectly legitimate to vary the shape to suit your design. Do any appliqué or embroidery on these vestments before making them up.

On the pattern diagram, each square measures 2 inches, or 5 centimeters. This means that the dimensions of the vestments will vary slightly according to which system of measurement you use. With the inch measurement, the back of the chasuble will measure 50″ from the back of the neck to the hem. The front will measure 46″ from the front of the neck to the hem.

If you use the centimeter measurement, the back of the chasuble will measure 125 cm and the front 115 cm.

(NOTE: The measurements given on the pattern diagrams allow for the curve of the neckline, and therefore are the *total* length of fabric you will need for the front and back.)

To make a chasuble, stole, burse, and veil from this pattern you will need 4¾ yards, or 4.40 meters, of fabric. These measurements include just under half a yard, or 45 cm, of extra fabric for insurance when cutting out. *Add ⅝″ (or 1.5 cm) seam allowances to all pattern pieces.*

Directions for Making Chasuble

a. Make paper patterns for the back and the front of the chasuble. If you need to lengthen or shorten the robe, do this at point A-B. Fold your fabric in half and lay the center front and center back along the fold. Add the seam allowance and cut out.

b. Cut the lining the same size as the chasuble, but then cut off ¼ inch (6 mm) all around the outside edge. This will prevent the lining from sagging below the edge of the garment.

c. Machine-stitch the shoulder seams on both chasuble and lining and stay-stitch around the neck and outside edges on your stitching line, as this will make it easier to turn the seam allowance under.

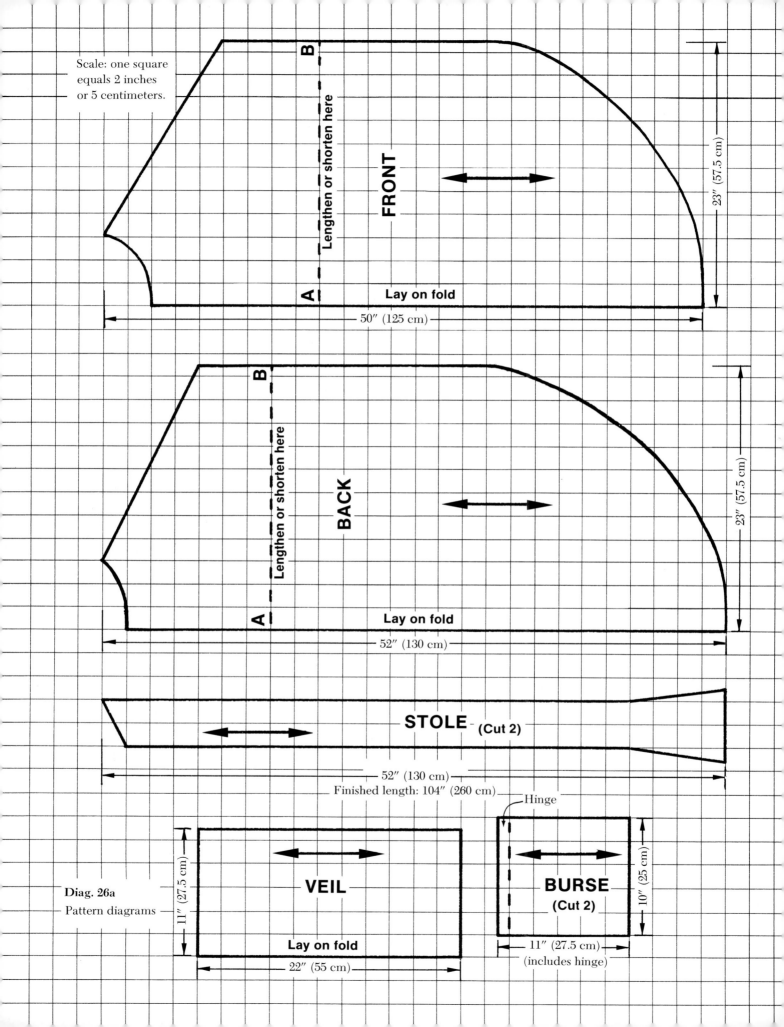

Scale: one square
equals 2 inches
or 5 centimeters.

B

Lengthen or shorten here

FRONT

A   **Lay on fold**

23″ (57.5 cm)

50″ (125 cm)

B

Lengthen or shorten here

BACK

A   **Lay on fold**

23″ (57.5 cm)

52″ (130 cm)

STOLE (Cut 2)

52″ (130 cm)
Finished length: 104″ (260 cm)

Hinge

VEIL

Lay on fold

11″ (27.5 cm)

22″ (55 cm)

Diag. 26a

Pattern diagrams

BURSE
(Cut 2)

10″ (25 cm)

11″ (27.5 cm)
(includes hinge)

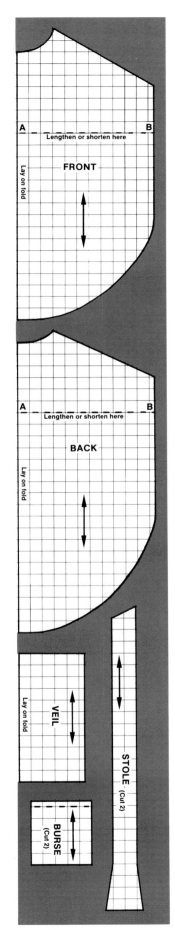

Diag. 26b

Pattern cutting layout

d. Place the lining over the chasuble *right sides together* and seam around the outside edge, thus forming a bag. Turn the chasuble right side out through the neck opening and press. (You may wish to baste these outer edges before pressing in order to ensure that the lining is "rolled" under.)

e. Turn in the neck seams and hand-stitch the lining in place.

It is possible to buy dress fabrics these days in a 60-inch (152 cm) width, which is, of course, more economical, but furnishing fabrics are seldom made in a 60-inch width. A firm that specializes in wide fabrics for vestments in spun silk or wool is G.J. KilBride (see fig. 6). Their fabrics are handwoven and hand-dyed and drape beautifully, and they would be suitable for a conical-shaped chasuble. They do mail order and their address is: G.J. KilBride, Cefn Cottage, Llanfair Croes, Abergavenny, Gwent NP7 9DE, Wales, U.K.

Directions for Making the Stole and Chalice Veil

a. The width of a stole is a matter of taste, and the length will vary according to the height of the wearer. The diagram shows one half of a narrow stole measuring 4″ x 104″, or 10 x 260 cm, with wedge-shaped ends that will extend a little below the hem of the chasuble. Cut out, adding seam allowances.

b. For making up the stole, seam together the two parts at the neck (the angled seam enables the stole to sit comfortably at the neck), then follow directions b) and d) above, leaving a small opening in a side seam to pull the work through to the right side.

c. The dimensions of the chalice veil given in the pattern are 22″ x 22″, or 55 x 55 cm, but these may vary according to the height of the chalice. Make up the veil following the directions for the stole.

Directions for Making the Burse

a. Cut two fabric squares as shown in diagram 26a, adding ⅝-inch (1.5 cm) seam allowances on all sides. Trim 1 inch (2.5 cm) from the top edge of the *front* piece only. This will then give you a hinge on the *top* edge of the back piece. Cut two squares of lining fabric the same way. Cut four squares of cardboard 10″ x 10″, or 25 x 25 cm.

b. Appliqué or embroider a design on the front fabric.

c. Place one square of cardboard in the center of each square of fabric and of each piece of lining. Then carefully glue the seam allowances over the cardboard, leaving the hinges free. Miter the corners and snip away part of the seam allowance at each side of the hinge in order to eliminate bulk (diag. 27). Use a fabric glue that dries without leaving a mark.

161

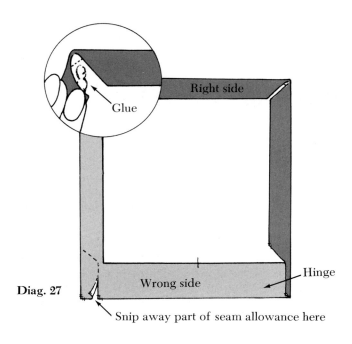

Diag. 27

Right side

Glue

Wrong side

Hinge

Snip away part of seam allowance here

d. Sandwich a top square to a lining square and invisibly whipstitch together. Leave the *top edge of the burse front open* in order to insert the hinge (diag. 28).

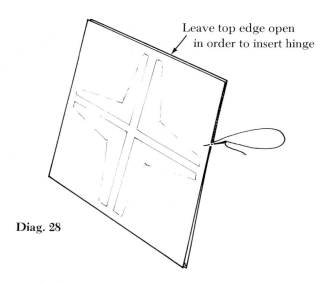

Leave top edge open
in order to insert hinge

Diag. 28

e. Insert the hinge down the top of the front square and pin (diag. 29a). The burse should lie flat when it is closed, so if it does not lie flat, you may have to loosen the hinge a fraction. Hem the top edge and lining closed (diag. 29b).

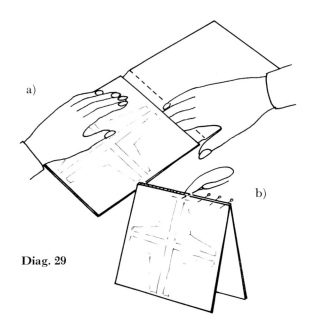

a)

b)

Diag. 29

Christian Signs and Symbols

Christian religious symbolism appeared in the catacombs of Rome as a code for communication and recognition between members of a persecuted sect. One of the earliest symbols was the fish (see fig. 4). Other symbols were the dove, the ship in full sail flying before the wind, and the anchor. Later on in the Middle Ages, symbolism was used as a means by which to illustrate Bible stories and themes to a largely illiterate population, and to convey an understanding of God. It was an early form of audiovisual teaching aid. Christian signs and symbols borrowed heavily from paganism and from other faiths, notably Judaism.

The Cross, which is now the universal sign of Christianity, did not appear in art until the reign of Emperor Constantine in the third century A.D. The emperor's mother, St. Helena, who was reputed to have been a humble innkeeper's daughter from Bithynia (in present-day Turkey), became an enthusiastic convert to Christianity and set off at the age of seventy-two for the Holy Land. She discovered three crosses in a cistern under the temple of Aphrodite. One was identified as the True Cross after St. Helena had performed a miraculous cure by placing it over the body of a dying woman. The other two crosses were said to be those of the two thieves who had been crucified on either side of Our Lord.

The Crown of Thorns also appeared as a symbol of Christ's suffering in later times. Although it is mentioned in three of the Gospels, the Crown of Thorns is not mentioned in the early writings of the church. St. Louis (1214–1270), the famous crusader King of France, was given what he believed to be the original Crown of Thorns by a grateful Emperor of Byzantium during one of his crusades, and he bore it triumphantly back to France, where it became the most important relic in his personal chapel, the glorious Sainte Chapelle in Paris. In fact, the "crown" was just a wreath of rushes, but it caught the imagination of European artists, who began to depict it in paintings of the Crucifixion from the mid-1200s. An explanation of how the popular monogram of Christ, the Chi Rho, came into being can be found in the caption for figure 2, and the meanings of many of the other traditional symbols appear in various other captions for the color plates.

Symbols are, in a way, the alphabet of Christianity, and new forms of calligraphy have been created throughout history, reflecting the prevailing artistic styles and feelings. The artworks in this book show some striking new symbols that have been created to reflect contemporary thought as well as national and geographical characteristics, flora, and fauna. Those of you who are creatively inspired may wish to originate signs and symbols of your own.

Some of the artists, whose work you have seen in the color plates, have kindly allowed me to reproduce their contemporary designs in diagram form. You will need to turn them into patterns, and an explanation of how to do this is given below. However, if you use these designs in your work, please remember to credit the artist in any public showing or publication. I have included some traditional symbols as well, but there are many books on the market that will give more of them.

How to Make Patterns from the Diagrams

Each diagram can easily be enlarged on a photocopier, so determine the size you need and take the measurements with you to the photocopying shop. Do it in sections, if necessary, and tape the sheets together. Some photocopiers distort, so you may have to adjust some of the lines by hand.

Because of the danger of distortion, pieced patterns *must be drawn up on graph paper to ensure accurate templates.* If you find this difficult, ask the photocopying shop to enlarge the pattern on tracing paper. Place the tracing paper over a piece of graph paper of the appropriate size and mark the divisions. Correct lines with a ruler.

To make templates, trace each pattern piece on plastic or cardboard.

Please remember that you may only use such photocopies *for your personal use*, otherwise you infringe the law of copyright.

163

1. *Angel.* This pre-Raphaelite angel appeared on the Christmas banner designed by Gill Bryan in figure 44b. Gill adapted her design from a drawing by Bev Saunders. Crinkly wool was used for the hair.

2. *Angel.* Dora Velleman appliquéd her enchanting angel on the net fall that hangs in front of her magnificent lettered pennants in figure 88b. She also put more angels on the back of the pennants.

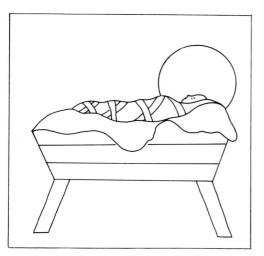

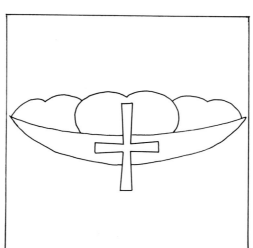

3. *Baby Jesus.* From the Christmas banner by Gill Bryan (fig. 44b). The covering that overlaps the manger was cut with scissors to create the effect of straw.

4. *Bread and Basket.* Gill Bryan placed this symbol of the Eucharist in the center of a divided cross on her green altar frontal in figure 40a. You could adapt the design to represent a basket of five loaves for the Feeding of the Five Thousand (Matthew 14:13-21).

5. *Bulrushes.* Bulrushes symbolize the hope of salvation for the faithful, a reference to Moses in the bulrushes and to Job 8:11. Gill Bryan depicted them on her lovely baptistry banner in figure 42b.

6. *Butterfly and Cross.* Barbara Rickey chose the *cross fleurée* for her banner in figure 75a. She placed a butterfly in the center as a symbol of the Resurrection.

7. *Candles.* This charming pieced pattern of Advent candles appears in the top left corner of the 275th anniversary quilt designed by Dorothy Sime in figure 80. The block was made by Lynn Perekslis.

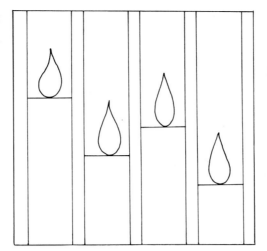

8. *Chalice.* A symbol of the Eucharist, but the Sabbath and chief Jewish festivals are also consecrated with bread and wine. (See Genesis 14:18.) A chalice with a silver serpent is the emblem of St. John the Apostle.

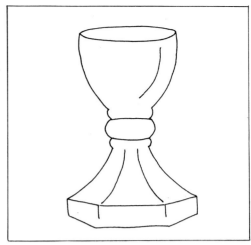

9. *Cross.* Elma Kramer chose Celtic braiding for her altar set in figure 82b because it has no beginning and no end, and is therefore symbolic of the eternal significance of the Cross. Celtic interlace is associated with early Christianity in Ireland and Great Britain.

10. *Cross.* Gill Bryan designed this divided cross for her contemporary altar frontal in figure 40a, and it was made up in two colors—yellow-gold and red.

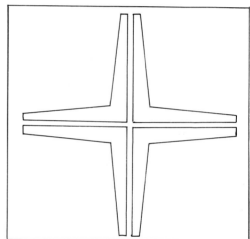

11. *Cross.* This was the cross that Sister Josephine Niemann, S.S.N.D. designed for her processional banner in figure 66c. It was appliquéd on mosquito netting to allow the free passage of air.

12. *Cross.* Pamela Hardiman designed a strip-pieced cross for her inspiring quilt in figure 118, but her cross was adapted by Sister Josephine Niemann, S.S.N.D. for a funeral banner, and it is this adapted version that is reproduced here. It is a Four Patch pattern.

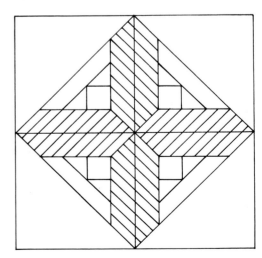

13. *Crown.* The first crowns were probably wreaths of flowers or leaves that were worn on the head as an emblem of victory. Now they symbolize regal authority.

14. *Crown of Thorns.* Although mentioned in three of the Gospels, the Crown of Thorns did not appear in religious art until the thirteenth century, when St. Louis brought back a relic in the form of a wreath of rushes from the Holy Land.

15. *Dove.* A dove is used as a symbol of the Holy Spirit, and it was one of the first Christian symbols. Here is Donna Garofalo's graceful dove from her hanging in figure 71.

16. *Dove.* Barbara Littlechild used a more contemporary dove on her Pentecost banner in figure 44a. The outline was couched with speckled wool.

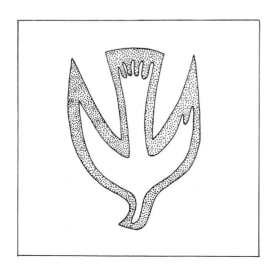

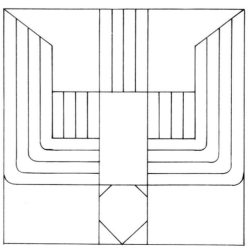

17. *Dove.* Here is an interesting dove done in outline form. It was designed by Doreen Walker and appears on her banner in figure 47.

18. *Dove.* Nancy-Lou Patterson designed this striking pieced dove for her Pentecost banner in figure 87. It was made up in shades of white and gray.

19. *Flames.* Flames are also associated with Pentecost, and these were designed by Barbara Littlechild (see fig. 44a). If you make them, remember that real flames usually have some blue in them.

20. *Flaming Torch.* Torches like this one are used as a symbol of the light of the Gospel, and often appear on emblems associated with well-known saints.

21. *Fish.* These are the fish that Gill Bryan placed on her altar frontal in figure 40a. Fish are an early symbol of Christianity, and they are also associated with the Feeding of the Five Thousand (Matthew 14:13-21).

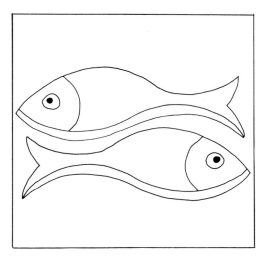

22. *Fish.* The Holy Trinity is usually expressed by a triple motif. Here are three entwined fish that in some ancient bas-reliefs are mounted within a triangle, itself a symbol of the Trinity.

23. *Fleur-de-lys.* The *fleur-de-lys* is also a symbol of the Holy Trinity, and is often associated with the Virgin Mary because it is a stylized form of lily.

24. *Grapes.* These clusters of grapes were taken from John Plume's handsome pennant in figure 43d. You could use them in an allover design or as a border pattern. Grapes look much more realistic if they are made from a variety of fabrics.

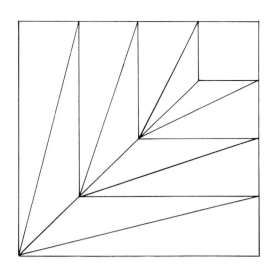

25. *Hosannah*. Here is the traditional American pieced pattern that Carole Riffe cleverly adapted for her altar frontal in figure 62.

26. *Ivy*. Ivy is associated with Christmas, but it also symbolizes life eternal. John Plume hand-painted the shaded areas of these leaves with yellow fabric paint. See his striking design in figure 43b.

27. *Lamb*. This is a modern interpretation of the well-known symbol Agnus Dei (Lamb of God), holding the banner of victory, which you often see in stained-glass windows. "Behold the Lamb of God that takes away the sin of the world" (John 1:29).

28. *Lamp*. Lamps are traditional symbols representing Jesus as the Light of the World, but a lamp like this one could also refer to the Parable of the Wise and Foolish Virgins (Matthew 25:1-12).

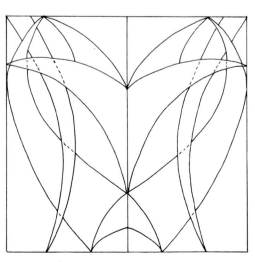

29. *Lilies*. These are Gill Bryan's attractive lilies taken from her banner in figure 42a. Lilies are a symbol of purity and therefore a symbol of the Virgin Mary. Sometimes you see them associated with the Archangel Gabriel.

30. *Lily*. This is the fascinating abstract lily pattern designed by Gerry Enger for the border of her banner in figure 77a. It is an appliqué pattern, and one half is the mirror image of the other.

31. *Palm.* Palms are associated with Palm Sunday, of course, but they can also represent spiritual victory—for example, a martyr's triumph over death.

32. *Passion Flower.* Passion flowers appear on the beautiful banner designed by William Phinnie and made by Connie Brooks and Jeanette Conrad in figure 76a. The blossom contains all the symbols associated with Christ's Passion.

33. *Peacock.* The peacock stands for Christ's Resurrection and Immortality, symbolized by the annual shedding and replacement of the bird's plumage. A fine peacock can be seen on the banner in figure 76c, designed by William Phinnie and made by Jeanette Conrad and Judith Logan.

34. *Pelican-in-her-Piety.* The pelican became a symbol of Christ the Redeemer because early naturalists believed that a female pelican would pierce her breast in order to feed her young with her own blood. William Phinnie used a similar version on his banner in figure 76b.

35. *Pomegranates.* Carolyn Clough designed these pomegranates for her contemporary banner in figure 43a. The outlines of the seeds were embroidered in black wool. The pomegranate is a symbol of the Resurrection, and because of the number of seeds it contains it can also represent the church.

36. *Rose.* This charming pieced Christmas rose was designed by Aase Pedersen and Kirsten Dissing Overgaard for the frontlet in figure 29a. Roses and daffodils are used as symbols for Christ in Europe.

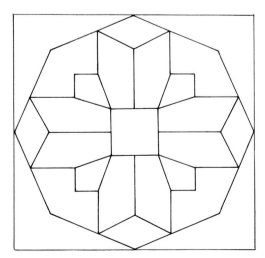

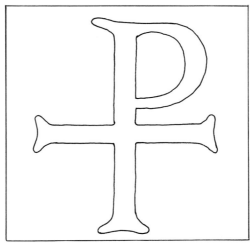

37. *Sacred Monogram Chi Rho.* This version of the Chi Rho (pronounced Ky Ro), the monogram of Christ, was used by Deborah Melton Anderson on her lovely altar frontal in figure 63.

38. *Sacred Monogram Chi Rho.* Here we can see another version of the Chi Rho that Jennie Parry made the centerpiece of her colorful altar frontal in figure 39a.

39. *Sacred Monogram Alpha and Omega.* The letters Alpha and Omega are the first and last letters of the Greek alphabet and are symbols of God (see Revelations 1:8). Robert Plouffe put them on his stained-glass banner in figure 78.

40. *Shepherd #1.* This shepherd appeared on Gill Bryan's attractive Christmas banner in figure 44b, which was adapted from a card designed by Bev Saunders.

41. *Shepherd #2.* With all these shepherds, you will find it easier if you make one complete template for the basic robe, and then apply the capes and outer robes separately on top.

42. *Shepherd #3.* Different types of wool were used for the hair of each shepherd and fake lambskin was used for the sheep. The crossbands and patches may look fiddly to do, but they do add interest to the figures.

43. *Ship*. A ship in full sail on the sea of life is one of the earliest symbols of the church. This one was designed by Joyce Harris for her handsome pulpit fall in figure 82c.

44. *Star*. Stars are essential for any depiction of the Nativity and are notoriously difficult to draw. Here is one for you to enlarge.

45. *Wheat and Poppies*. Gill Bryan included poppies in her pennant design (see figure 43c) in order to introduce some color, but poppies are rarely found in Christian symbolism. Wheat, of course, is the symbol for the Eucharist.

46. *Wise Man #1*. This wise man can be found on Gill Bryan's Christmas banner in figure 44b. It was adapted from a design by Bev Saunders. A real tassel was used on the hat.

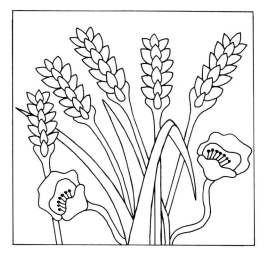 

47. *Wise Man #2*. This particular wise man was given a dark complexion in Gill Bryan's banner, and silver tissue was used for parts of the robe.

48. *Wise Man #3*. Make the robes of all these Wise Men like those given in the directions for the shepherd in diagram 41. We used fake silver and gold leather for the three incense pots.

Notes

1. Quoted in article in *Canada Quilts,* Grimsby, Ontario, Vol. XVI, no. 4, 1987, page 8.

2. John Julius Norwich, *Byzantium* (London, England: Viking, 1988), page 40.

3. Marion P. Ireland, *Textile Art in the Church* (Nashville, Tennessee: Abingdon Press, 1966), page 59.

4. Catalogue of J. Whippell and Whippell Mowbray Church Furnishing Ltd., Exeter, England, 1989, page 20.

5. Ed. Elizabeth Ingram, *Thread of Gold—The Embroideries and Textiles in York Minster* (Andover, England: Pitkin Pictorials, 1987), page 12. Quoted in the introductory essay "Ecclesiastical Vestments at York Minster Before the Reformation" by Sylvia Hogarth, page 12.

6. Ibid., page 12.

7. Ibid., page 30.

8. *Encyclopedia Britannica,* Vol. 19, page 40.

9. Robert Bishop and Elizabeth Safanda, *A Gallery of Amish Quilts—Design Diversity from a Plain People* (New York: E.P. Dutton and Co., Inc., 1976), page 22.

10. Joyce D. Hammond, *Tifaifai and Quilts of Polynesia,* (Honolulu: University of Hawaii Press, 1986), page 30.

11. Averil Colby, *Patchwork,* London: B. T. Batsford, 1958, pages 143-144.

12. Dronning Margrethe 11, Skitser og fædige arbejeder 1970–1988 (Køge Kunstforening: Kunstmuseet Køge Skitsesamling, 1988), page 14.

13. Ibid., page 14.

14. Ibid., page 15.

15. Søren Lodberg Hvas, *Dronningens Kunstværk* (Haderslev, Sœrtryk af Haderslev Stiftsbog, 1988), page 24.

16. Ibid., page 18.

17. Quoted in the book by Aymar Embury II, *Early American Churches* (Doubleday, Page and Company, 1914), page 7.

18. Ibid., page 11.

19. Ibid., page 14.

20. Robert T. Hardry, *A History of the Churches in the United States and Canada* (Oxford: Clarendon Press, 1976), page 183. (This book is part of a series called The Oxford History of the Christian Church.)

21. Ibid., page 258.

22. From information kindly supplied by the Reverend Dr. G. Carroon, Archivist-Historiographer of the Episcopal Diocese of Connecticut.

23. G. Sherington, *Australia's Immigrants* 1788–1978 (Sydney: George Allen & Unwin, 1980), page 23. (Quoted in *Patchwork Quilts in Australia* by Margaret Rolfe, Victoria, Australia: Greenhouse Publications Pty. Ltd., Richmond, 1987, page 18.)

24. Marion Fletcher, with the assistance of Leigh Purdy, *Needlework in Australia* (Oxford University Press, 1989), page 101.

25. Chaucer; *The Canterbury Tales:* Tr. Nevill Coghill, (Harmondsworth, Middlesex, England: Penguin Books Ltd., 1951), The Prologue, page 31.